The DarkSide

Wri
June Lundgren

Copyright 2015

Preface

This book is dedicated to those who seek the truth and are not afraid to ask questions. In all things there is a good and bad. There is light and darkness and in the darkness there is evil, an evil beyond human comprehension. In this book you will find some of the answers you seek about the dark side of the paranormal. No one has all the answers and nor should they because not knowing keeps us seeking the truth. The information in this book was given to me by beings of light and those in the angelic realm. It is meant to answer most of the basic questions about the dark ones for in knowledge there is light.

TABLE OF CONTENTS

IN THE BEGINNING

People are always asking me if demons really exist. Demons really do exist and I have been unfortunate enough to encounter several of them. To understand what a demon is we have to go back to the beginning of our existence on this planet. I'm sure you're all familiar with the battle between God and Lucifer.

Our souls have experienced many mortal lives over the centuries. Many millennia ago we had physical bodies as we do now. As time progressed, we evolved to the point of being pure energy. We traveled and explored the known and uncharted reaches of space. We visited countless worlds watching the inhabitants' lives and progress.

Time and destination were irrelevant to us. We traveled in a group made up of billions of individual soul consciousness. We existed in relative harmony for much of our journey of exploration. After exploring and traveling to the farthest reaches of the universe, most of us grew weary of traveling and longed for a place to call our own. It took us around three thousand years to find a planet that was suitable for our needs and able to sustain a carbon-based life.

Once we found our planet there arose a division amongst us. There were those who did not want to return to a physical existence, saying it was too limiting. They did not want to be confined to a shell-like body where they would be subject to a limited lifespan, unable to travel the stars on a moment's notice. They worried that once again we would be subject to physical weaknesses such as pain, disease, physical and mental disabilities, as well as all manner of temptations.

The souls were divided into two groups—one headed by God, the other by Lucifer and his followers. God tried to reason with Lucifer, telling him that he would never force him to take physical form. He promised Lucifer that it was entirely up to him if he chose to return to a physical body.

This was not good enough for Lucifer and in the end, a terrible battle erupted between the two sides. It was not a battle as you or I would think of it. There were no guns, swords, or weapons like in the physical world; rather they were battles where the weapons were pure energy and light. The battle raged on for over a thousand of our years, ending when Lucifer was defeated. There were no physical bodies to count, but rather the souls were lost because their energy was scattered between the spiritual plane and the physical world.

When the battle was over, Lucifer stood before God, still unswerving in his refusal to return to physical form. In the end, God gave Lucifer what he wanted; he would never to be able to return to physical form. He warned him that once this was set in motion there was no going back.

Lucifer and his followers would spend eternity as energy, never to return to be reborn into the physical world. As part of their punishment, He banished them from the light. The fallen angels were condemned to live in a realm of never-ending darkness. Lucifer, never thinking the time would come when he would want to return to a physical form, readily agreed to God's terms. You see, Lucifer was not always so terrible, but over the thousands of years living in darkness, his heart turned cold and cruel. He blamed humanity for his exile into darkness. After all, if the other souls had not wanted to return to a physical existence, none of this would have happened. He would not have been condemned to exist in a world of darkness.

From that moment of realization, he made it his goal to cause as much pain and suffering as he possibly could to humanity. He is constantly trying to turn as many souls as he can to the darkness, in an effort to punish God.

OPEN YOUR MIND

One of the most important things I have learned when dealing with the other side, whether it be the light or dark, is that you have to stop thinking like a living person. You need to move beyond the physical world and enter a world where energy, whether it's light or dark has its own set of rules. I know you're asking yourself, what does she mean by this and I'll elaborate.

First throw out everything you think you know about the paranormal. In the physical world we are subject to the laws of physics. In the other planes of existence physics as we know it do not work. They have different type of psychics which work very differently than ours.

Let me give you an example: We use our imagination to move beyond reality where anything and everything is possible. We can create new worlds filled with people and places. We can travel to the stars, explore other worlds and even move forwards and backwards in time.

Our imagination is the first step in making the impossible seem possible. In the other planes of existence telepathic energy is used to accomplish actions. As with the physical body we need thought to send the impulses to the brain in order to do just about everything. In the other plane its much the same except there is no physical body to use.

They use thought to travel from one dimension or place to another. Since our souls are made up of pure energy there are no physical restrictions. Each plane of existence resonates on a different energy level and requires a change in resonance to travel from one plane to another. Its kind of like having an electronic locking system with an optical scanner integrated into the locking mechanism. Entities of light and dark resonate on different vibrational frequencies. Entities of light vibrate on a high-frequency. Entities of darkness vibrate on the lower frequency and we are somewhere in between.

These planes are protected, but once in a while a negative will break through using a back door, so to speak. By back door I mean a dark portal or with the help of a living person. This can happen in three ways:

The *first* way to enter our world is a portal is opened. This can happen in one of three ways:

During a séance or use of an Ouija board

Through satanic rituals
Dark Portals

People who perform séances and use Ouija boards to contact the dead without knowing what they are doing are an accident waiting to happen. If these people who open the portal don't close it then negative entities as well and good entities can enter our world through the portal.

Most of the time the people who have opened these portals do not realize they have opened one, let alone know how to close it.

The *second* way negatives can enter our world is by a person performing satanic rituals. The person opens a portal to bring forth a demon or some other servant of the dark one. Whether by accident, stupidity or on purpose they neglect to close the portal once it is open.

The *third* way is by the use of a dark portal. These dark portals are created by demons from the other side. The veils (walls) that separate our world from the next are very thin. I liken them to shear curtains which you can see through but are very delicate. Once you get a run in these curtains a hole can form. Once a hole is formed these negatives can work to and enlarge the hole so that they might pass through it. This creates a dark portal.

As the negatives pass through the portal the vibration of the portal changes so that it becomes a dark portal. These dark portals are almost impossible to locate. They are well camouflaged but every now and then I find one. And when I find them Michael the Archangel helps me to close it. Once it's closed by an Archangel it cannot be reopened. I know that eventually they'll create another one but they'll have to work hard to create it.

FEAR OF THE DARK SIDE

Fear of the darkness and what lies beyond is at the very core of human consciousness. Since caveman days we have feared the dark and what lies in wait there. For centuries man has shied away from talking about the evil ones and in doing so has created even more fear of them. Fear of talking about the dark ones only leads to greater fear. It is your fear of them that will draw them to you.

Even today in many cultures it is taboo to speak about the dark side. People are afraid that in mentioning negatives you will be bringing attention to yourself and make yourself a target for them. I have spoken with people that have different types of spiritual practices such as Rikki healers, followers of Solomon and some Wiccan practitioners.

In doing so I have found there is a great and natural fear connected with the dark side. I understand their feelings and misgivings completely having dealt with the dark ones for the last twenty-five years. There are those people who believe that if you write or read about negative entities, you will draw them to you. These people believe that once you delve into the information, whether it be reading, writing or even watching a movie, you open yourself up for attack or attachment by these creatures.

Some Rikki Masters teach their students to fear talking about anything negative such as demons, Satan, shadow people or negative earthbound spirits. They believe in speaking these creatures names you have opened yourself up to the dark ones. They are right about one thing; you never want to ask a demon's name unless you are ready to do battle with it.

It has been my experience in dealing with the dark side, just talking about the dark ones will not draw them to you. They don't need any help in finding you if they want to. Negative people attract negative entities just as positive people attract positive entities.

The one thing that most people fail to understand about the dark side is all creatures from the dark side can see the future. They know your future, they know if you are going to become a light worker for God or do great things to help humanity. This is what they want to prevent. They will try to turn you away from God to the darkness. They may put roadblocks in your path to prevent you from achieving your goal to help humanity.

If they can turn a light worker to the dark side it is quite a feather in their hat. They use deception as their number one tool.

They will make you doubt yourself, your abilities, faith and even God himself. If that doesn't work they will try to lure you with promises of, wealth, love, fame and in some cases revenge. Each time they turn a light worker towards the darkness they gain more power.

CREATURES OF DARKNESS

Did you know that the dark ones have two different names? Yes they do, one born of light and one born of darkness. The name of light for the dark one is Lucifer the name of darkness is Satan. They all have them but to name the others would not be safe, suffice to say the ones that I have encountered in the physical world I have always gotten names for but will not repeat. There is a hierarchy even on the dark side which plays out something like this:

•Lucifer is the leader, he is the oldest and strongest of the fallen angels. His name translates into 'the shining one'.
•High Demons- the equivalent of what I call the old ones in the angelic realm (Moses and the old profits such as Elisha).
•Lesser demons are equivalent to the Apostles
•Shadow people- creatures of stealth and shadows
•Minions and lesser creatures there are several types of these creatures
•Negative earthbound spirits- nasty in life and nasty in death.

Most of these entities are at their strongest during the hours of darkness, which makes total sense as they are creatures of darkness. Do not underestimate them, even at their weakest they are ten times more powerful than a living person. They have the element of surprise on their side because most people can neither see, hear nor sense them.

Some people think that if they don't believe in these creatures then they cannot be hurt by them. While others believe that if they just ignore them they will go away. I say to those people, they are living in a fantasy world. You may not believe in the dark ones but they certainly know of and believe in your existence.

The worst thing you can do with these entities is under-estimate them. It is the worst kind of mistake to believe that you know everything there is to know about them and how their world works. That sort of thinking will either get you hurt or killed. Even as long as I have been working with the dark side I still don't know everything about their world.

To fully understand it you would have to enter their world and I am not willing to do this. There is one archangel who willingly entered the dark realm, Azrael. He entered their realm to try to save those who were willing to turn away from the darkness. He and a few others who believed in his mission are there to this day. God allows this in the hope of saving a few souls who honestly want to change.

There are three main types of negatives which I will cover in this book.

• Demons,
• Lesser demons,
• Negative earthbound spirits.

When most people think of negatives, they think of three distinct types: shadow people, demonic and earthbound negative spirits. These negative creatures are not limited to the afore mentioned three. In this first book I will discuss their type, but never their name. I had someone who was working in a television studio during one of my appearances, come up to me and ask what some of the names of the demons were. I told him that to mention their name was to invite demonic attack and attachment.

I would caution anyone thinking of dealing with these entities not to. Because unless you have strong faith in God, have been taught how to do it or are a holy person with a lot of experience. If you think you have a demonic problem find someone who is experienced in the art of identifying and removing these creatures.

Not just anyone can deal with these creatures, it takes someone with strong faith, experience and special abilities to be able to withstand an encounter and cast them back where they belong. You should never deal with a negative on your own, you should always ask for intervention from God.

As mere mortals we are not equipped to deal with these creatures on our own. We need divine intervention, because to deal with these entities without the divine is to invite defeat in so many ways.

WHAT ATTRACTS CREATURES
OF DARKNESS TO A PERSON

In the dark ages the church believed the only cause for these creatures to seek you out was if you were practicing witchcraft or sorcery. There was no such thing as an innocent person being plagued by these creatures. You must surely be guilty of one of these transgressions.

Who can say with absolute certainty what attracts these negative creatures to a person. Sometimes it may be that you're just in the wrong place at the right time. You may be drawn to a building or a location where a negative dwells such as a house, piece of land, an old road, vehicle or an object such as a vase, picture or mirror.

We know now that even those people of intense faith can become targets for these creatures. The dark ones do not discriminate, everyone is a potential target. There are things that draw or attract these creatures to people. I have listed below some of the main reasons which can leave you open for this. Here is a list of some of the situations which can draw a negative to a person?

•Substance abuse
•Weakened faith or doubtful faith
•A near death or out of body experience
•Severe depression

•Mental illness
•Always dwelling on the negative side of everything
•Delving into witchcraft or Satanism
•Chaos or extreme disorder in a person's life
•Fear
•Paranoia
•Living in clutter and disarray
•Holding séances or using Ouija/ Witch boards
•Paranormal investigations done without protection
•Fascination with dark entities
•Having to deal with the darkness on a regular basis-i.e.: performing exorcisms, house clearings or cleansings.

These are some of the things that I have found to be true in my 30 years of dealing with the dark side and also some of the information I have received from the archangels.

IS IT REALLY A DEMON?

Is there a way to tell if the entity is really a demonic? For people with psychic abilities most of the time it is easy to tell. At other times the entity may cloak itself while observing the living, waiting for its chance to cause problems. When it does this you may sense a negative presence but not be able to tell what kind it is.

The *first* way is all about how you feel. A ghost will make you feel cold externally, i.e.: cold spots, a cold breeze or a chill out of nowhere. Demons make you feel cold inside, it's a core coldness that has nothing to do with the external ambient temperature. You may also experience nausea, overwhelming anxiety, and the smell of rotting flesh or sulfur which seems to permeate the air. The air will feel heavy and thick making you feel like its hard to breathe.

The *second* way to tell if the apparition of a person or animal standing in front of you is a demon is their eyes. If you really look into their eyes you will see a golden glow behind them. It is like seeing the reflection of a candle in someone's eyes. It is often said that the eyes are the windows to the soul and in this case they truly are. It will also be painful for you to look into their eyes, kind of like staring into the sun, it hurts to look at them.

The *third* is by commanding the entity as follows: "In the name of Jesus Christ I command you tell me the truth, are you a demon? What do you want? How many are you?" the entity will be compelled to answer you truthfully or it may just vanish from our plane of existence. They are not going to communicate with you if they can help it. You must be forceful in your commands, like you have every right to command them and expect an answer.

My grandmother Edith had just such an encounter as a young woman.

Edith as a young woman lived in Hutchinson, Kansas. In the town in the 1920's there was a house that was rumored to be the most haunted in the town. Atchison, Kansas, is proclaimed to be the most haunted town in Kansas. But in the 1920's Hutchinson had its own haunted reputation.
One night she was out with a few friends and one of them suggested going to the house to see if the rumors were true.
"What are we going to do tonight, this town is so dead." Cathy, my Edith's best friend asked.
"Hey I've got an idea lets go over to that old house over by Fred's house." Ralph suggested.
"You know the one Cathy, the one everybody says is haunted."
"I know the one, but I'm not so sure about going inside. I get the hee-bee-gee-beez just walking by the place."

"What a great idea," George said excitedly. "Maybe we can find an open window and get inside."

"I don't think that's such a good idea George." Edith interjected.

"You're not chicken are you Edith?" Ralph asked smiling.

"I just don't want to get into trouble that's all." Edith said. But was actually thinking, 'Oh lord I know that place is haunted and I don't want to go anywhere near it.'

"That's set then, let's go" Ralph said grinning wickedly at the others.

They piled into George's car and drove over to the house. Arriving at the house Edith started feeling sick to her stomach. She could sense a evil presence lurking inside the old dilapidated turn of the century house.

Ralph and George circled the house trying to find a way in.

"It's no good," George said, "we'll just have to jimmy the lock on the front door."

"Okay, let's do it." Ralph said and together they tried to open the door but were unable to. "Well it looks like we're not getting inside."

Cathy spoke up from behind them, "What about that window?" she asked pointing at the window on the far end of the porch.

Everyone turned to see the window was actually open a jar.

"That's strange I checked that window myself and it was closed." George said. Shrugging he walked over to the window and forced it open crawling through. Once inside he opened the front door and let the others inside.

Pausing at the door she Edith took a moment by herself and silently asked for God's protection before entering the house.

Everyone started exploring the house, but Edith remained close to the door. She could feel the presence watching them. It was plain that none of the others were aware of the presence, and since she did not want them or the entity to know of her abilities, she said nothing.

A sudden flurry of activity seemed to move through the house. Books and papers were flying off shelves; objects were thrown across the room. Cathy screamed, "Its haunted, I told you we shouldn't have come. I saw something black moving across the room." Edith could hear her shouting hysterically.

She heard Ralph and George trying to calm Cathy down. They were trying to tell her it was the wind.
Distancing herself from the others, Edith closed her eyes and opened her senses, trying to locate the presence.

After a moment or two, she opened her eyes and found herself drawn to the second-floor landing. Slowly climbing the stairs, she could feel the entity watching her. As she reached the landing, the presence she had felt earlier manifested itself in the form of a black shadowy figure.

Drawing a deep breath, she confronted the entity and asked, "In the name of God, what do you want?" She knew that the entity would have to either answer the question or disappear from walking the earth.

There was no answer; instead, the black shadow form disappeared before her eyes. With the disappearance of the entity, Edith could feel a lightening of the atmosphere in the house. She never returned to the house, and shortly after that, she moved to Chicago.

SIGNS

There are always signs of an active demonic presence, you just need to be aware enough of your surroundings to take notice. Here are some signs of demonic presence:

•The number three or things done in a series of three, such as three scratches, taps or knocks. They do this to mock the trinity of the Father, the Son and the Holy Spirit.
•Any one of these types of infestations: flies, spiders, mice, birds or rats. These are simply creatures which are easily manipulated by the dark ones. They have no regard for these creatures, they just enjoy tormenting and killing them. They will even make birds fly into doors and windows so that they die.
•The smell of sulfur, rotting meat, rotting flesh, decay or the stench of death. It is the most putrid and offensive smell in the world.
•Animals will be fearful and not want to go anywhere near anything negative. You should be very aware of the animals around you, both inside and outside of your home. They are a great indicator of paranormal activity, especially negative activity. Just as animals are drawn to angelic beings whenever they are present, these same animals are repelled by the presence of a dark entity.

•You will experience nightmares, but these nightmares will seem so real that when you wake you are not sure what is a dream and what is real. These nightmares always center on death and violence to yourself or loved ones. The negatives may appear in the guise of a loved one who has crossed over.

DEMONS
THE OLD ONES
And
LESSER DEMONS

Appearance

Not all demons try to hide what they are, most of them enjoy showing their true form to the living. In doing this they can elicit absolute fear in whoever sees them which they can feed from. These demons are always the most powerful ones. They have no fear of the living including holy people. I call these demons the old ones.

These particular demons have been around since the beginning and are the most powerful of all the negatives except for Lucifer. They rarely waste their time entering our world, but when they do its because they have something to do for Lucifer. These demons are ones you do not want to run into.

Lessor demons will try to gain your trust they do this in order to gain control over you They want to make you dependent on them. Once they have gained your trust they will start influencing you to do things that seem harmless at first. They will start out with small things and work their way up to influence you to do things you know are wrong. Before you know it you are under demonic influence or oppression.

These lessor demons never travel alone they always travel in packs. There is a dominant demon and at least one or more minions. If you can get rid of the main demon the others will flee. The minions I liken to pilot fish that feed off of the leavings of sharks. They attach themselves to the lessor demons and serve them.

Most people think of demons in connection to darkness and night time activity. Some people think these creatures are weaker during the day and stronger at night. This is a myth; they are just as strong in the daylight as they are at night.

Granted the darkness is the perfect cover for their form and nocturnal activities. The only difference is that they can't hide in the light of day. If you can see them coming at you there may be time to prepare yourself for their assault.

Their appearance for the most part is always the same. They choose to appear in the following forms:

•Half animal, either goat, ram, bull, snake, bat, spider and half humanoid.
•Black shapeless mass
•Invisible except for red or gold eyes
•In extreme cases they will take on the form of Jesus or God with yellow glowing eyes to mock them.

Abilities

Demons all have the following abilities some to a lesser degree than others.
•They can read your mind.
•Put thoughts in your mind. They have even been known to influence people to commit suicide or murder.
•Cause you to feel negative emotions such as depression, anger, jealousy, fear and even paranoia.
•See the future. Like angels, these creatures can see your future. The ironic part is they can't see their own.
•Possess a human body giving it super human strength, levitation, manipulate objects, teleportation.
•They can pick up objects, no matter how heavy, including people and throw them.
•They can cloud the mind of most people so that you cannot see or sense their presence.
•They can cloak their presence from the living and sometimes from the archangels.
•Disguise themselves as a friend, loved one or shadow person.
•They can trap other earthbound spirits whether good or bad and torture them.
•They can kill people and animals- they like to prolong the death of the person or animal causing as much pain and suffering as possible.
•Suck the life force from a living being.
•You might hear voices, growling, screams and insidious laughter.

•Your sense of smell and even taste can be affected.

•Cause you to suffer unexplained health problems.

•They can and do affect the physical world in many ways: they have been known to start fires, throw objects, turn on lights, stoves and any electrical devices.

•You may be physically attacked by scratching, hitting, pushing, and shoving.

•In extreme cases possession of your physical body can occur. When this is done your consciousness is pushed to the back so that you are aware of what's going on but are powerless to stop it. When it has possession of the person's body the person can exhibit super-human strength, aggression, levitation of the person and objects and speaking in dead languages.

The worst thing that can happen to a person is possession in one form or another because it is harder to deal with. There are different forms of possession, these include the following:

Oppression-
1. Abnormal, irrational fear
2. Abnormal, irrational anxiety
3. Abnormal, irrational loneliness
4. Lack of self-control
5. Conflicts with authority figures
6. Aimlessness; the feeling that life is void of any meaning or purpose

7. Depression that is not physiologically induced.
8. Outburst of hatred
9. Violent behavior
10. Loss of the fear of God
11. Selfish ambition (appetite for power)
12. Irrationality

Infestation- This is when a building, property, objects, (cars, electronic devices, stoves) and even animals are affected and react out of character.

Partial possession- is when the demonic will possess the person's body and mind sporadically. The person's consciousness is pushed to the back and the demon takes possession. The person can see what's happening but is powerless to stop it.

Full possession- This is when a demon (or demons) take full possession of the person's body and mind. the person is completely unaware of what is happening.

If you should come across anyone with these symptoms then the only thing you can do is get them to a priest, because no one in the physical world will be able to help them.

The only entities who can help the person is Jesus, God and an Archangel. The most feared is Michael, Auriel, Gabriel, Raphael, Ezekiel and Azrael.

Can A Demon Be Contained?

I have heard some people think you can catch and contain a ghost or a demon in some sort of trap. There is a television show on right now with a paranormal group from down south who are trying to catch a ghost or a demon in a trap.

They have tried to capture one using a mirror, batteries, solar units and even a trap shaped like a pyramid. Each time they are certain they have caught something. Once they think they have something in their trap they take it back home with them to find out what they've caught.

I don't know about anyone else but my home would be the last place I would take something with a negative entity in it. The trap always ends up being empty. And it's a good thing too because what would they do with it once they caught it? I don't think they've really thought this through.

While these guys are in the building they have a meeting and talk about what they plan to build and how they plan to trap the entity. News flash boys, the entities are not deaf, dumb or blind, they can hear every word you say. And even if they couldn't, they can read your minds!

You can bind a ghost or negative earthbound spirit to an object or a piece of land but you cannot trap one in a trap.

There is nothing in the physical world that can contain or entrap a demon. There is only one way to contain a demon in the physical world and that is by using an infinity orb. There are three requirements for being able to create an infinity orb.

•You must first find someone with the soul of an archangel.
•This person must be aware and accepting of who and what they are.
•The person must be able to link with their soul and other souls from the angelic realm.

Unless all three of these requirements are met the person will be unable to create what Michael the archangel calls an infinity orb.

These orbs are made up of pure white light energy and can be used to trap, contain and send the negative entity back where it comes from. Archangels also use these orbs sometimes to transport negative earth bound spirits to limbo, where they are released into a type of isolation booth. When the soul is in the booth they can see and hear everything that occurs but no one can see or hear them. They can yell, get mad and have a fit in absolute silence.

They are usually put there to reflect on the pain, suffering and negative actions they caused during their last life time. They are left alone and the archangels who monitor the chambers check on them from time to time to see if they are truly sorry for what they have done. If they have truly changed then they are assigned a job to do to make atonement for what they have done during that life time.

If they are not sufficiently repentant then the archangels will know and the soul will remain there no matter how long it takes. It is impossible for them to lie to the archangels who oversee these booths because they will know if they do. Michael has told me that there are some that have been there for several hundred years.

Once in a great while there will be a soul that will not repent. If it does not after a reasonable amount of time then they will be brought before God and given one last chance before they are relegated to the darkness. These souls are far and few as souls know the consequence of their actions can lead them to be cast into the darkness or worse, completely destroyed.

Can Demons Be Destroyed?

There are varying opinions on whether a demonic can really be destroyed. Some believe they can never be destroyed only sent back into the darkness. While others believe that a holy person can destroy them.

Usually they are cast back down into the darkness but occasionally will have to be completely destroyed. Lesser angels can and do contain the lessor demons, shadow people and minions.

In this chapter I will attempt to answer the following questions:

•Can demons be destroyed?
•What happens when a demon is destroyed?
•Who can banish a demon?
•What happens to the entities when they are destroyed or banished?
•What does an exorcism do?

A Lot of people believe demons cannot be destroyed only sent back to the darkness. This is not true, demons can be destroyed but not by a normal mortal.

Demons can be destroyed by God, Jesus, archangels and a mortal with the soul of an archangel. These archangels in physical form are rare and at this moment in time there are only eight in the physical world. Demons are only destroyed in extreme cases. Here is an example of one such instance:

Hitler was a follower of the occult and had practiced satanic worship. During the beginning of his fanatical quest for power he summoned a demon, a very old, very nasty one. This demon was accompanied by 2 lesser demons. These demons influenced Hitler and his closest men to commit atrocities on innocent people. Michael was sent to capture the old demon and bring it back for judgement by God.

The demon was captured and sentenced to death for what it had done. Auriel carried out the sentence and the demon was destroyed by her plunging her flaming sword. (This sword was actually made up of white light energy but appears to us to be flames).

Demons can be banished from a location by preforming a whole house exorcism or by an exceptionally powerful medium, with strong faith in God, holy person or a demonologist.

When a demon is destroyed it ceases to exist on any level. Its molecules are spread among the stars. When it is banished it is sent back into the darkness where it will remain until once again it finds its way back into the physical world.

The ritual of the exorcism is done to remove a demonic who has taken possession on an individual. Whole house exorcism's can be performed on a house or a building. You can also have an exorcism done on an object or a piece of land. This should be done by someone trained in the art of exorcism because if you fail the consequences would devastating.

Demons can be destroyed but not by anyone in the physical world unless they have the soul of an archangel. They can be destroyed by Jesus, God, or an archangel. It is only in extreme cases that a demon is completely destroyed. When they are destroyed it is not like a death of the physical body where the life force is released and we are once again pure energy.

I have only seen the destruction of a demon once and it is not easy to explain so I'll try to explain it in a way that is easy to understand. Here is what I was shown:

I was sitting having a telepathic conversation with Michael the archangel about dark beings.

"Can demons be destroyed and not just cast back down?" I asked him.
"Yes, they can be destroyed."
"How do you do it?" I asked curiously.
"Is easier if I just show you how its done."

Suddenly I was seeing Auriel the archangel wrestling with a demon. It seemed to go on forever then Auriel raised her arm and a flaming sword appeared in her hand. Bringing the sword down in one blow she sliced through the demon. It didn't bleed as you would in the physical world instead the demon disintegrated into what appeared to be a fine powder.

The scene before me vanished and it took me a few moments to digest what I had just witnessed. Once I could think coherently I asked Michael about it.

"So what did I just see?"
"You just witnessed Auriel battle a demon and destroy it." He said matter of factly.
"I know that, what I want to know is what the fiery sword was all about."
"Each of us, archangels have a fiery sword that we use to dispense justice or retribution as the condition warrants. In this instance Auriel used it to destroy the demon. The demon was a very old and powerful one. It was a demon that influenced the mass destruction of thousands of Jews during the holocaust."

*"I'll bet it was one of the 'old ones'". I said.
"Just before the time of the holocaust Jesus was reborn in physical form. He knew what was to come and wanted to experience the holocaust through the eyes of a young Jewish child. He was 12 years old when he was killed at Auschwitz. He was then able to inform his father of his experience and a judgement was made against the demon. Auriel was sent to carry out punishment."*

*"Who makes the judgement call?"
"The decision is made ultimately by God but Jesus is allowed to weigh in and his opinion is considered by God before judgement is handed down. Jesus then has the job of assigning a archangel to carry out the judgement. The job always falls to an avenging angel. At the time Auriel was an avenging angel."*

"Why Auriel? Why not Ezekiel, Raphael or even you?"

"That's a very valid question. In your world you have elite snipers called hitmen. They are the best of the best at what they do, eliminate the target. Auriel was known as the best hitman we had, even better than me, which is saying something. This demon would not be easy to find and once you find it, you need to eliminate it."

"Don't you know where the demon is? Why do you have to search for it? I would have thought it would be easy enough to find it."

"If it's out of the dark realm then it's easy to track, but if it's in the dark realm we have to wait for it to leave. We are forbidden to enter the dark realm without the express permission of God."

"Well how do you track it then? Do you just think of it and zero in on it?"

"It's not quite that simple. We can sense it but they can also sense us. We both have the ability to cloak ourselves and therefore it makes it hard to track them."

"It's a wonder you ever find them at all then. So how do you find them without them finding out?" "That's where you come in. Not you specifically but you as a living person." He said smiling, but I wasn't sure I liked the way he was smiling.

"I don't think that I like the way you say that. What do you mean by that?" Then a thought occurred to me, "Hey, you don't mean you're using us as bait? You did that to me once and I didn't like it!"

"Well most humans are clueless in regards to the dark ones, you and a few others like you have the ability to see them even when they're cloaked. That's why every person with your abilities has an archangel assigned to them. It's kind of like an early detection system, if you can sense them then we can sense them through you."

"Wow", I said sarcastically, "that makes me feel really good."

"When a demonic or other negative soul is destroyed, the energy that was the soul is dispersed among the stars and it no longer exists as a sentient entity."

"You mean its completely destroyed, there's nothing left of who or what it was?"

"That's right, the energy that was contained within the soul is broken down on the molecular level and it ceases to exist."

"How often does something like that happen?"

"No, it is only in extreme cases such as genocide or mass murder that judgement is passed and the soul is destroyed."

This was the first and only time so far that I have seen a demonic destroyed. A person with the soul of an archangel can help facilitate the destruction of these creatures. A normal human being cannot do this, not even a priest.

Weaknesses
And
Fears

Do demons have weaknesses? Do they fear anything or anyone? These are questions that anyone who has to deal with demonic entities would like answers to.

You would think that something as powerful as a demon would not have any weakness or fears, but they do. Up until now little has been known and even less written about this subject. Guardian angels and guides are on the front lines so to speak. They are with us every day so they know when a mortal encounters a demonic and the information is instantly relayed to the archangels. This is how the archangels track the movements of cloaked negatives. Just as archangels can cloak themselves so can the negatives. Neither one of them can cloak themselves completely there is always a faint residual energy that surrounds them.

Once the demon is found its activities are monitored by the archangels. If the demon is causing problems with the living then an angel is sent to monitor the situation and report back to Ezekiel. Ezekiel makes the decision with regards to who is sent to dispatch the demon.

I asked God to send me someone who has knowledge of negatives and knew everything there was to know about them. The information that I am placing in this chapter was given to me by Ezekiel and Azrael. These archangels were sent to help me write this book and they are a couple of the oldest of the demon slayers.

Fears

Everyone has fears of one kind or another, demons and their minions are no different. The only reason you don't hear about them is because they hide their fears in a deep dark place.

•All demons have an innate fear of Jesus, God, angels and archangels in particular. The reason behind this is because once an angel knows where a demon is, then the archangels know where it is. It is archangels who have the ability to not only cast them back into the darkness but also to destroy them.

•Archangel Michael- For years I have known demons fear Michael, the archangel, more than any other archangel. It wasn't until ten years ago that I found out why. They fear him because he was the one who dealt the final blow that disarmed Lucifer and ended the war.

•Auriel- They fear Auriel because she took down the second in command during the war, Lucifer's son.

•They fear their destruction, (death) more than we as humans do. When we die there is another plane of existence waiting for us. But when demons are destroyed they cease to exist at all. For them there is no longer any kind of existence or consciousness. What's left of their soul energy is spread among the stars.

•They fear the white light of God, (power) because with the light comes the fear of exposure to archangels. The light brings the power of God and Jesus with it against the entities of darkness.

•The image of Jesus strikes fear in them because his power like Gods is all powerful and whenever the name of Jesus is invoked to defend against a negative it calls archangels to the person who is seeking his help.

Weaknesses

Most people think that demons don't have any weaknesses. People believe they are all powerful, but this is not true. When you come in contact with a demon it will try to find your weaknesses and use them against you. I have felt for a long time that people need to know what I have learned over the years of dealing with the dark ones. The information contained in this book has been verified by the archangels.
•Their greatest weakness is their hatred for those who condemned them to the darkness. God, Jesus and the archangels.

•Revenge against the souls of light who helped to incarcerate them in the darkness. Its strange to me that they should seek revenge when it was their own doing and Lucifer in particular who they should blame. They made the decision to start the war and so should not blame anyone but themselves.

•Their superior attitude and absolute belief that they have the right to control mortals and that we are lower life forms.

• They have an inability to see their own future have which has lead them to some major defeats.

•They like a lot of mortals they judge all mortals by the physical appearance of a person instead of what's on the inside. Its only when they are on the losing end on the battle that they start to look for what's beneath the surface and by then its too late for them.

•They judge all mankind by the actions of a few weak, stupid, greedy ones, and in doing so they make mistakes. Unlike most people they don't learn from their mistakes, they keep repeating them over and over. I think this is why the archangels call them stupid.

•They do not like blessed objects including holy water and anointing oil as it weakens them.

SHADOW PEOPLE

Is there such an entity known as a shadow person? Were they once living breathing people or are they something darker, more sinister? Is it just an urban legend or a figment of our imagination? Where do they come from and why are they here? Can they hurt us, and if so why would they want to? Why is it that most people don't seem to know where they come from? How do they enter our world? Why do they appear in certain places and not in others?

In the following chapters I will answer these questions and many others. The information in these chapters are from my personal encounters as well as validation from those on the other side.

Since the beginning of recorded history there have been references of these shadowy creatures in every culture. Some call it shadow creatures, skin walkers, doppelganger. Whatever name you give them they are nasty. They remind me of vampires, they move in the shadows mostly under cover of the darkness. They stock their pray learning their weaknesses and fears. Once they have learned all they can about their pray then they move in for the kill.

There are several theories about what or who these creatures are but no one has been able to say for certain just what they are. One theory is that they are demons and have never had a human existence. A second theory is they are the negative part of a person's soul which is left behind after the person dies. The last theory is that they are ghosts like any other except they are particularly nasty.

From the experiences I've had with shadow creatures I have found there is a grain of truth in each one of these theories. My guides have confirmed the information that I have included in this chapter.

Shadow people do exist, just ask anyone who has had an encounter with one of them. They are linked to Lucifer, but each one is an independent entity. They maintain an active link to the darkone in much the same way as the angels maintain their link to God. They are a type of dark minion and like so many of the creatures of darkness, thrive on negative emotions.

What separates them from other negatives is they not only feed off the negative emotions but also the very life force of a person or an animal. Their sole aim is to collect souls, cause pain, suffering and devastation to the living as well as earthbound spirits. I know from personal encounters that they are extremely dangerous to any living being whether they are human or animal.

Appearance

The appearance of these creatures for the most part doesn't vary. One thing remains constant they are always solid black looking. They can change their shape from a human like form to a black fog, mist or blob. People have reported seeing shadow people with grotesque mask like features. Others report seeing two large red eyes staring at them from a black humanoid type form.

Upon rare occasion they will show themselves to the living as something harmless, such as a child. I have experienced this myself, here is what happened. (Excerpt from my book Paranormal Encounters).

Most of the time psychics and mediums can see through the projected appearance that ghosts like to present. At first, we may perceive them as they want us to see them, but soon the illusion drops away and they are revealed for what they really are. It can be as frightening for them to see us as it is for us to see them. My most recent encounter with a shadow person was when I went to the coast for a couple of days.

Shadow Person

It was the week of Thanksgiving 2011; my husband and I decided to visit my cousin who lived at the Oregon coast in Newport. Her husband was ill and could not come up for Thanksgiving, so we decided to take Thanksgiving to him. We were able to book a room with our timeshare at Schooner Landing in Newport.

The first night we were there my husband and son were downstairs in the living room area and I was upstairs in the master bedroom. Suddenly I felt a chill and started looking around for the cause of it.

"June, get down here!" I heard my husband shout.

Jumping up from the bed I hurried down the stairs. My husband was standing in the living room staring into the dining area.

"What's that?" He asked me in a hushed voice. Looking in the direction he was staring, at first I saw a childlike figure. What I saw was not in correlation with what I was feeling. The sense of dread and feeling cold to my core was a clear indication of a negative entity.

"Mom, what is that thing? I don't like it, it makes me feel scared and I want to throw up." My son said keeping his eyes on the figure.

"It's not what it appears to be, it's not a child. It's a negative entity I need to look deeper to see its true form." I told him. I decided to expand my protective shield around my husband and son before unmasking it. Concentrating on the entity I began to see what was hidden behind the childish mask. It tried to keep me from seeing its true form. Every time I would get close to seeing what it really was it put up another barrier. At last I managed to see what it really was, a show creature.

Staring at it intently I said, "You need to go back where you came from, now." The minute I voiced the command it turned, looked at me and showed its true form for all to see. In the instant I thought to banish it, it read my thoughts and disappeared out of the condo through the sliding glass door.

Visibly shaken my son asked, "Was that one of those shadow people? That's the same feeling I got when I went into that ceramic shop in Damascus. I could hardly wait to get out of there. I made myself stay and look around to see if I could find it and I could feel it following me."

"You should have had you're protection in place or let me know when you go so I can extend mine around you. The demon that resides there is attached to the land not the buildings."

"Well if that's any indication of what they can do, I don't want to see another one! It gave me the creeps and made me feel sick to my stomach." My husband said.

I looked at him with a slight smile and said, "Welcome to my world."

I headed back upstairs to the bedroom where I found my sister sitting on the bed. "That creature certainly chose the wrong place to be didn't it? No telling what kind of mischief it would have gotten up if I hadn't influenced Dan into going into the kitchen for a snack."

"I was wondering why he noticed it; it's so unlike him to notice anything paranormal."

"Well I figured it wouldn't hurt him to get a little taste of what you have to deal with. Maybe he would be a little more understanding of what you have to go through. As for Ray, he needs to be aware of what those creatures look like, so that he will know to steer clear of them in the future."

"What's up with that shadow person? Isn't it unusual for a shadow person to take on the façade of a human? They usually don't try to hide what they are, that's more of a demonic trick. I've never heard of them showing themselves as anything other than what they are. Why do they use the pretense?"

"It couldn't sense your presence at first and was caught off guard when it saw you. It tried to hide by taking on the form of a child. But once it could sense the presence of a light being, meaning Michael, it tried to hide from him by showing itself as a ghost instead of what it really is.

Those creatures will never learn that we're far too clever to be fooled by them, stupid creatures." She said shaking her head.

"Remember what your grandma told you, 'just when you think you have the other side all figured out, you don't'. Never think that you know everything there is to know about the paranormal. I can tell you right now, even with all your knowledge and experience, you haven't seen everything the dark ones can do. For that matter you haven't seen everything that we can do either."

"I understand that you can't think like a human in dealing with the shadow people. You're not bound by laws of psychics like we are here on this plane of existence. What can a person do if you can't protect yourself against a physical assault?" I asked her.
"You're still thinking like a human, you have to think like them. If they can shove or scratch you using the energy they project, you can do the same. You have to believe and learn to use the energy that is a part of you. All living things have energy fields and different vibrations; you just have to learn how to manipulate the energy around you as well as your own energy. If you're strong enough you can use their energy against them."

"And are you guys going to teach me how to do it? Because, if not, it might take me a while to figure out how I can use their energy against them."

"Yes, we'll teach you how to do it. It's not something you can learn overnight it takes practice. It is well worth learning; very few humans have the knowledge, and ability to do it." From that day forward I started keeping a protective barrier around myself.

Abilities

Their usual method of operation is to incite fear in the person thereby producing negative energy to sustain themselves. They do this by allowing glimpses of themselves in various forms and reaching into your mind at night giving you nightmares.

These creatures can read your inner fears and they will appear to you in one of their forms that will elicit the most fear from you. Most of the time the entity will appear at night. They can suck the energy from a being over a long period of time. They do this to sustain themselves and to prolong the suffering of the living.

The person or animal will experience:
•Nightmares
•Restless or fitful sleep
•Noticeable drain in energy
•The victim may become depressed
•Suicidal
•They can strangle, suffocate, and choke you
•Cause illness and decline in health
•Stress a person's heart and even cause the death of a person or animal

Children, animals, elderly, mentally unstable and the infirmed are particularly vulnerable to these negatives

If you have any animals in your home you will either need to keep them somewhere else or close by your side every moment of every day. If you don't they will become unwilling victims of these creatures. They will kill and torture them just for fun.

They can and will project images into your mind and make you see things that do not exist. They can also appear as something harmless, but most of the time they do not bother covering up what they are. They know what you fear and use these weaknesses to their advantage. To show fear or lose faith is to invite an attack or worse. Shadow creatures do not usually travel in pairs or groups as demons do. They are solitary creatures preferring to have their own territories to themselves. It is unusual for there to be more than one in a location.

When you do find more than one it is time to have a whole house exorcism performed. A cleansing will not get rid of these beings; it will only make them angry.

Can They Be Contained?

Shadow creatures cannot be contained within anything in the physical world. They can be sent back into the darkness using a portal, but unless the portal is closed after the creature passes through it, it will return.

The only way it can be contained is within an infinity orb just as a demon can be contained in the same manner.

They can be bound to an object like earthbound spirits can be. But why would you want to do this? Just because they are bound to an object does not mean they have no power to affect their surroundings. Anyone or anything within their general vicinity can and will be affected by them unless the object is surrounded by a line of salt, preferably black salt.

Can They Be Destroyed
Or Removed?

To remove these creatures you will have to call
on a clergy, medium or a demonologist.
Sometimes in extreme cases it may take a
higher power such as an archangel or Jesus.

The medium or demonologist, must be a person
with strong faith, strength of will and absolute
belief in what they are doing. This should never
be attempted by anyone who has not been
trained.
A protective barrier should always be placed
around you before you attempt facing the
shadow person. Shadow creatures can sense
your fear or your lack of faith. Don't think you
can catch these creatures unaware. They know
you are coming even before you know.

They will always try to shake your faith in
yourself and in God. Even if they know you are
strong enough to defeat them, they will still try to
frighten and intimidate you. They do not give up
easily and neither should the person doing the
removal.

If a whole house exorcism is done by a demonologist or a medium and fails, you must then find a clergyman who is willing to do the exorcism. These are harder to find, it is a specialty that not all clergy men are trained or willing to do. Every priest, reverend, shaman, and pastor only gets basic instruction in how to perform an exorcism. The Catholic Church has priests specifically trained in the art of exorcism.

Fears And Weaknesses

Like all other negatives shadow creatures have fears and weaknesses. Little has been known about these beings but in speaking with Ezekiel and Azrael the following I have learned what they know about these shadow people as most call them.

Fears
•Complete destruction or death of their consciousness.
•The light of God and Jesus
•Angels —especially archangels

Weaknesses

•Positive energy and thoughts deplete their energy.
•They judge mortals by their own shallow standards.
•They travel alone
•Think they are superior to light workers and humans
•They never look into the soul of a person only into the persons mind. Therefore they are unable to see the true power of the soul.

EARTHBOUND NEGATIVE ENTITES
SPIRITS/GHOSTS

A ghost is a person's soul that is released from the physical body but does not ascend completely to the other side. The reason a soul may not ascend can be due to one of a number of reasons:

•Traumatic death
•They felt they were not ready to die
•They are filled with anger, guilt
•The person was negative, controlling and angry in life and angry that they have lost control
•They may have left something unfinished or do not want to love a loved one

If the soul does not fully ascend but remains earthbound then it retains the same mindset and character as it has in life. If they were nasty in life they will be nasty in death until they fully ascend.

Appearance

Earthbound spirits will usually appear as they looked in the physical world. I liken this to as they said in the movie the Matrix, residual self-image.

If the death was sudden or traumatic the spirit may be stuck in their death state. This means they will appear as they were in the moment of their death. If they were killed in an accident and their body was covered in injuries then this is how they will appear. Once they move past the moment of their death only then will they be able to move on. Sometimes even though they move past the moment of their death they are still unwilling to fully ascend.

Like other negatives they can change their appearance. In life they may have been short, balding, nasty and controlling. In death there is no limit to what they learn to do. They either learn from trial and error or they are taught by other entities. They can show themselves as seven feet tall, as a shadow person, demon, child, friend or even an animal. They may seek to control, scare and even seek revenge on the living.

Abilities

Most people believe ghosts can't hurt you only demons can. That's where they're wrong. All spirits have the ability to interact with the physical world in some manner. The more advanced they are, the more they can affect the living physically, emotionally and mentally. By this I mean that they are able to effect the living in the physical world.
Like the other negatives they can:
•Read your mind
•Put thoughts in your mind, such as suicide and harming someone. They have even been known to influence people to commit suicide or murder.
•Cause you to feel negative emotions such as depression, anger, jealousy, fear and even paranoia
•They can move objects, no matter how heavy, including animals and people.
•They can cloud the mind of most people so that you cannot see or sense their presence.
•Give you nightmares
•Disguise themselves as a friend, loved one or shadow person
•Make you physically ill to the point that you may experience debilitating illnesses.
•They can trap other earthbound spirits whether good or bad and torture them.
•They can kill people and animals.
•You might hear voices, growling, screams and insidious laughter

•Your sense of smell and even taste can be affected

•They have been known to start fires, throw objects, turn on lights, stoves and any electrical devices.

•You may be physically attacked by scratching, hitting, pushing, and shoving.

•In extreme cases possession of your physical body can occur. When this is done, your consciousness is pushed to the back so that you are aware of what's going on but are powerless to stop it.

Can They Be Removed
Or Contained?

A negative entity can be removed by anyone if the entity is not too advanced and not too nasty. If the spirit is too advanced or too nasty then you will need to get professional help.

If the spirit is not too advanced, there are a couple of ways you can try to remove it.

•Try to communicate with the spirit by sitting down with the house quiet and acknowledge the spirit. Let the spirit know it is dead. Tell the ghost it no longer lives in the home, building or land and that it belongs to you now. Ask the spirit to leave and cross over into the light.
•You can smudge the home or building commanding the spirit to leave.

If the spirit is advanced then doing any of the above will have absolutely no effect. The only response you are likely to get is that to make it mad and there for make matters worse.

If you find that you have to deal with an advanced earthbound negative, you should be very careful. As I said before these negative entities can and will make your life a living hell. In order to remove an earthbound you will need one of the following:

- A medium
- Priest
- Shaman
- Wiccan
- Voodoo practitioner
- Demonologist

An earthbound spirit cannot be contained in a physical vessel of any kind. But the spirit can be bound to an object.

The only way a spirit can be contained is in an infinity orb just as a demon or a shadow person can be.

I would never bind a spirit to an object because I feel that the spirit should be released to cross over into the light. Even if the earthbound spirit is negative it can be released by an angel and taken to limbo where it will spend the time it needs in isolation.

Weaknesses And Fears

Negative earthbound entities like any other negative have their own weaknesses and fears. Below is a list of some of the most common.

Weaknesses
•One of their greatest weaknesses is they continue to think like a physical being.
•They are subject to the same emotions of anger, jealousy, control, greed and hate.
•After they die they have to learn how to do things as a spirit. For example move objects, make themselves heard and so on. This is not something they know automatically. This leaves them vulnerable to other more advanced spirits or demons praying upon them.

Fears
•Their biggest fear is Judgement for the evil they have done in their physical life. They feel as long as they stay earthbound they will not be subject to condemnation from God.
•They have a fear of being cast down into the darkness. They feel that staying earthbound is better than being cast down.
•They fear losing the control and power they had acquired in life

MYTHS ABOUT PROTECTION

There are a lot of myths and folklore about what works in the physical world for protection. Most of the things that people believe will protect them against demons and negative entities just don't work.

Some of the things I have seen in the paranormal TV shows are just ridiculous. Not only do they not work some of them are harmful to animals as well as humans. I have verified the list below with Michael the archangel to make sure that it is correct.
Here is a list of some of the things that people have been told to use for protection against negative which do not work:

•**Brake dust**- this is an old wives tale and I have never seen it actually work as protection or to ward off spirits let alone demons.
•**Tar water**- this mixture is hardly used anymore and the chemicals used in this is harmful to humans and animals.
•**Crystals**- they cannot protect you but can act as an early warning system, nothing more- the vibrational harmonics they give off will change- become lower when a negative is present.

•**Talisman, amulets and figurines**- cannot be used for protection unless they are blessed. And a figurine of the Grimm Reaper will actually attract negative energies. Paintings or cards with a rendering of Christ on them will not ward off negativity unless they are blessed and even then their protection is limited.

•Statue of the **Virgin Mary or any other saint**- unless blessed will not ward off evil. So they are of little protection.

•**Hanging the Eye of Horus or a pentagram** over the entrance of your house- will attract the spirits you are seeking to ward off.

•**A plain cross**-will not protect you it must have the representation of Christ on it.

•A lot of people think by **ignoring the entity** or **saying that you don't believe** in negatives will keep you safe. There is nothing farther from the truth.

•**White candles**-they will call angels near whenever they are lit but the candle in itself is not a protection.

•**Sage** is not a protection against evil. It will help to remove negative energy and in some cases the sage will remove a negative earthbound spirit, but it is too powerful they may come right back.

PROTECTION AGAINST
THE DARK SIDE

I truly wish the above mentioned things would work for protection, but unfortunately most of them do not. I know this from not only my personal experience but this information has been confirmed by the Archangels Ezekiel, Azrael and Michael.

Here is a list of things that will ward off and protect you from negatives:

Crucifix with the image of Jesus - not an abstract rendering.
Holy water- use to bless objects, animals, homes and people.
Black Salt- this is more powerful if you add sandlewood to the mixture- It is used to draw a line of protection around a person, place or thing. You can also carry it on yourself, put it in your car for protection.
Bible- reading scriptures will help to weaken the negative.
Sandlewood- burning pure sandlewood in any form will help to weaken the negative.
Archangels- all angels can protect you against evil. But to vanquish evil ones you will need an archangel.
Prayers- invoking the name of Jesus and God will help to protect you but will not keep them away permanently.

Michael the Archangel- asking God to send Michael to vanquish the negative is a powerful incentive for the negative to leave as they fear him above all other archangels. Here is a strong prayer to invoke his help:

St. Michael defend us in battle. Be our protection against the wickedness and snares of the Devil. May God rebuke Him we humbly pray O prince of the heavenly Host. By the power of God thrust into Hell Satan and all Evil Spirits who wander through the world for the ruin of Souls. (Created by Pope Leo XIII in 1886 in the Leonine prayers)

I would love to tell you that there is an absolute sure fire way to ward off negatives but I would be lying. The best way is to be aware of what is going on around you. If something doesn't feel right about a person or place then remove yourself from them. If you get a gut feeling not to do something or go somewhere then listen to that feeling.

Don't let your brain talk you out of it, If you feel something dark around you, sick to your stomach, feelings of dread and anxiety, feeling like someone is watching you and there is no explanation for it, then get help right away. Go to a medium, priest or holy person to have your home and yourself blessed.

Too many people will put off finding help thinking they can deal with it themselves. This is the worst thing you can do because it gives the negative time to get a hold on your life and family. If your children suddenly start to have imaginary friends when they have never had them before, then ask them about the friends.

Sage your home and ask for God's blessing on your home. If this does not get rid of the friend then when your child is out of the house command the entity to "In the name of Jesus Christ and God to leave your home" you must be forceful and mean every word you say.
If this does not work then you will need a holy person to come in and bless your home and family.

AFTER THE ENCOUNTER

No matter what type of negative you deal with, there is always a trace of residual darkness attached to you after the encounter. This darkness will have to be purged after the encounter.

This can be done by prayer and bringing the white light of God into the crown of your head. Let the light fill your entire body and bubble over out of the top of your head.

If you are having to deal with the darkness on a regular basis either as a demonologist, paranormal investigator or because you work or live where there are negatives, this is something you will have to contend with.

When someone has been touched by the darkness by either having an attachment, infestation or oppression you will have to be extremely vigilant when it comes to the paranormal. Once the dark ones are made aware of you, they never forget.

I'm not telling you to obsess or think about the dark ones, quite the opposite. This type of scenario is one of the few times I can say that thinking of them constantly will draw them to you.

All I am trying to say is just be aware of your surroundings at all times and notice the changes in the atmosphere surrounding you in new locations or around new people.

If you have been affected by demonic possession, infestation or influence the dark ones know who you. These beings never forget who you are. This may sound a bit melodramatic but it is a fact. I have seen what the darkness can do to people it ruins all aspects of your life and those around you. These people are never the same after these encounters. The biggest mistake you can make after these encounters is to let fear rule your life. If you do then they have won and you will have a difficult life.

I am not saying everyone will be affected this drastically, but everyone will have problems for a while after the encounter. Sometimes a person will dwell on the past negative encounter so much that they will actually draw the negative to them.

HAUNTED LOCATIONS

What could cause a building or a piece of land to become haunted or have a demonic attachment? There are rare cases when a negative has been attached to a piece of land as far back as recorded history. In cases like this no one knows why it happens, you would have to face the demon and make it tell you why it is there. I have recently had such an encounter where I had to remove a demon that had been attached to the land since before recorded time. It was the first time I had encountered such a nasty old one.

Because I knew it was an old one I asked why it was there. It was not going to tell me but Michael forced it to. The demon told me it had gone against Lucifer. Lucifer cast it down into the earth and imprisoned it there. It had remained undisturbed until man encroached on its lair by building homes. It was interesting to find out the reason for its being in such a place.

Here are a few reasons for land and building based hauntings.
•   The land or place is the scene of a conflict or battle involving loss of life.
•   The site is associated with satanic worship or rituals
•   Buildings that have seen a lot of death like hospitals, asylums, prisons, jails, burial mounds and graveyards.

- Any site where people have been participating in multiple séances and using spirit boards to contact the other side.
- Any location where there is ongoing and frequent paranormal investigations by multiple groups.
- Anywhere the land has a demon dwelling underground.
- Any location with a portal attached to the land

Lightning Source UK Ltd.
Milton Keynes UK
UKHW021600280920
370666UK00008B/1902

THE WONDER TEAM
AND THE
FORGOTTEN
FOOTBALLERS

Other books by Leah Williamson

You Have the Power
Written with Suzanne Wrack

And coming in April 2024

The Wonder Team 2!
Written with Jordan Glover

MACMILLAN CHILDREN'S BOOKS

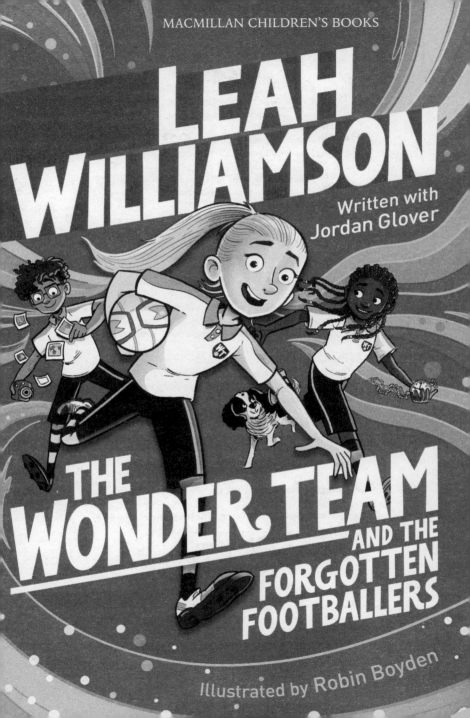

LEAH WILLIAMSON

Written with
Jordan Glover

THE WONDER TEAM
AND THE
FORGOTTEN FOOTBALLERS

Illustrated by Robin Boyden

Published 2023 by Macmillan Children's Books
an imprint of Pan Macmillan
The Smithson, 6 Briset Street, London EC1M 5NR
EU representative: Macmillan Publishers Ireland Ltd, 1st Floor,
The Liffey Trust Centre, 117–126 Sheriff Street Upper
Dublin 1, D01 YC43
Associated companies throughout the world
www.panmacmillan.com

ISBN 978-1-0350-2313-4

1 3 5 7 9 8 6 4 2

A CIP catalogue record for this book is available from the British Library.

Printed and bound by CPI Group (UK) Ltd, Croydon CR0 4YY

To our Uncle Nick,
who always supported our dreams,
and the dreams of many others too.

CHAPTER 1:
TIME TO STEP UP

The shrill squeal of a whistle sliced through the air. Puffing, Leah came to a stop. Miss Kaur had made them run farther than usual for their warm-up and Leah's entire body was tingling with warmth, despite the chilly January air. She brushed strands of sweaty blonde hair from her eyes as Mimi appeared at her side.

'Ugh, I'm not made for long-distance running, L. Especially on a Monday,' her best friend moaned, bending over and planting her hands on her knees. Her skin shone with a light layer of sweat.

'That's not true,' Leah said. 'You're a better runner than me. Much faster!'

'Faster. Yes. Further? No.'

Leah laughed and they joined the rest of the football team heading towards the benches.

'L! Mimi!' A familiar voice rang out across the pitch. Leah saw George, the third member of their trio, waving at them from the sidelines. He was bundled up in a thick black coat, his red bobble hat barely containing the wild brown curls dancing over his forehead. Leah and Mimi split from the other players and jogged over to meet him.

'Hey! What are you doing here?' Leah asked.

George grinned and held up a fancy camera, its exposed lens glinting in the watery winter sun. 'Miss Kaur asked me to take some pictures of your training sessions for the school newspaper. She wants to build up some hype before the big game on Thursday.'

'Don't remind me,' Leah groaned, covering her eyes with one hand. 'I've been trying not to think about it.'

'What are you talking about?' Mimi frowned. 'I thought you were looking forward to it.'

'I was, but after last week's match . . . I'd be

surprised if Miss Kaur even lets me start.' The corners of Leah's mouth turned down. 'I can't *believe* I missed that shot. She's going to bench me for sure.'

'You can't be perfect all the time, L,' George said. 'Everyone has bad days.'

Leah shook her head. 'Not this close to the end of the season, they don't. I've got to be on top form.'

George and Mimi exchanged a look, but before either of them could respond, Miss Kaur's voice drifted over from the benches. 'Come on, team!'

Leah and Mimi joined the rest of the players streaming towards their teacher. George followed behind, his camera at the ready. The team arranged themselves in a rough semi-circle around the bench, Miss Kaur at the centre. A football was tucked into the crook of her arm, her silver whistle hanging on a string around her neck.

She clapped her hands together. 'Right, you all know Thursday is a big game for us. Westfield High are a tough team to tackle.'

'Which is why we've never beaten them,' William Riley piped up. His beefy arms were crossed over his chest.

Miss Kaur tipped her head in acknowledgement. 'No, we've never won against them, but that's why this last training session is so important. It'll give us a chance to iron out our creases.' She paused. 'Look, I know you're all nervous about doing well, but you're some of the most talented kids I've ever coached. Compared to a few years ago, you're a wonder team! I know you can do this.' Reluctantly, the players nodded. Leah didn't think they looked very convinced.

Miss Kaur seemed to sense it too. She sighed and plucked up her clipboard from the bench, her eyes drifting down the page. 'Before we even start thinking about tactics, though, we need to get our final team organised.' She started to rattle off positions.

'Oh no,' Leah whispered. She looked at Mimi in panic. 'This is it. She's going to kick me off the starting eleven!'

'You don't know that,' Mimi whispered back

sternly, hands on her hips.

Leah gulped. She knew her friend meant well, but Mimi didn't understand. Leah's performance in the last game had been her *worst ever*. She'd been preparing for this moment ever since.

What if she cried? she thought suddenly. The thought was mortifying.

'Leah!' Miss Kaur's voice broke through Leah's thoughts. Her shoulders clenched as she braced herself for her teacher's next words. She tried to compose her face – she didn't want the team to see her shame and disappointment. She had to keep it together when Miss Kaur told her . . .

'You're going to be our primary penalty taker if that situation arises.'

Leah blinked. Next to her, Mimi whooped. There was a smattering of polite applause as Miss Kaur grinned at her astonishment.

Penalty taker? Did that mean she wasn't being relegated to the bench? Was Miss Kaur actually giving her a second chance? She couldn't believe it.

Neither could William. 'Her?' he spat in angry

disbelief. 'You can't be serious! I'm the top scorer on the team, not *her*. Besides, she's rubbish at penalties!'

'William,' Miss Kaur said, her tone thick with warning.

William snorted, shaking his head. 'The wonder team? More like the blunder team if you put her anywhere near the penalty area.' A few of the players around him sniggered, and Leah couldn't help the crimson flush that stained her cheeks.

'That's enough,' Miss Kaur said sharply. 'If you're going to argue with my decisions, you can leave my pitch. Is that clear?' William didn't reply, but he shot Leah a look of pure venom.

Leah's stomach writhed uncomfortably. William Riley was the worst bully in the school. Even most of the older kids went out of their way to avoid him. Now all of his attention was focused on Leah.

Miss Kaur shaded her eyes and she stared up at the sky. There was a shroud of dark clouds looming on the horizon that made her frown.

She chucked the clipboard back onto the bench, then threw the football to William. 'Let's get out onto the pitch,' she said. 'I don't like the look of that sky and I want us to get as much practice time as possible.'

As the team jogged onto the pitch, Mimi gripped Leah's arm, her face breaking into an excited grin. 'Leah!' she exclaimed. 'Penalty taker! This is awesome!'

'Is it?' Leah said faintly.

'Of course!' George had caught up with them. 'It's a big responsibility, but it shows Miss Kaur trusts you. Now, smile! I want to get a good shot for the paper.' He raised his camera to his eye, clicking the shutter. The smile on Leah's face felt false.

'George, Mimi, will you give me and Leah a moment, please?' They hadn't heard Miss Kaur come up behind them.

'Sure, Miss,' Mimi said, and she and George hurried off to where the other players were gathering by the goalposts.

Leah gulped as she was left with Miss Kaur.

She felt like her teacher was expecting her to say something, but she didn't know what.

Eventually, Miss Kaur said, 'Are you alright, Leah? I thought you'd be pleased to have been chosen as our penalty taker.'

'I am!' Leah blurted. It was true, especially because she'd been so sure Miss Kaur was going to bench her completely. 'It's just . . .' she hung her head. 'William's right. I *am* rubbish at taking penalties.'

'That's certainly not true,' Miss Kaur chuckled.

Leah continued as if her teacher hadn't spoken, 'And in our last game I missed that last shot. It was basically an open goal, but I bottled it!'

Miss Kaur's expression turned serious. 'Last week definitely wasn't your best game, Leah, but everyone has off days. A penalty taker doesn't always need to be the best goal scorer on the pitch. It's more important for them to be calm and collected, no matter what's going on around them. That's why I didn't choose William for this job.' She patted Leah on the shoulder. '*You* don't let your emotions get away from you. It's a great quality in a leader, and in a high-pressure moment a leader is what the team will need.'

Leah scrunched up her nose. A leader? *Her?*

Leah considered for a moment. *Was Miss Kaur right?* Leah knew that if she stepped up to this role, everything would change. It would mean being brave enough to take charge and tell people what to do, not to mention standing up and making big speeches.

She shook her head so violently that her ponytail whipped against the back of her neck.

'I can't.'

Miss Kaur's expression softened. She tilted her head to one side. 'I know this sounds scary, Leah. But I wouldn't have asked you if I didn't think you had it in you. It's time to step up to a new challenge.'

'What if I freeze again?' Leah asked, her voice dropping to a whisper. She hugged her middle, wrapping her arms around it.

Miss Kaur shrugged. 'Well, there's only one remedy for that. You'll have to practise! It's a good thing we're starting today's session with

some penalties, isn't it?' She grinned and nodded her head towards the rest of the team. Leah gulped, noticing the bag of balls slouched against the goalpost. She bit her lip. She felt dizzy and a little bit sick. *Could she really do this?*

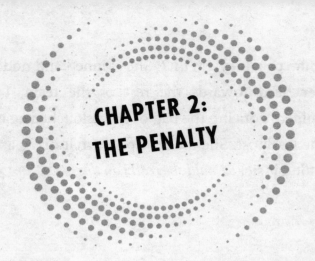

CHAPTER 2:
THE PENALTY

The decision was taken out of her hands as Miss Kaur placed her whistle against her lips and blew hard. Conversations died as the team turned their attention towards their teacher.

'We're going to warm up with some penalties today,' Miss Kaur declared, striding over to the bag of balls and beginning to pass them out amongst the players. Leah took hers reluctantly. 'Mimi, you can get us started.'

As the goalkeeper took his place in the middle of the net, Mimi danced up to the penalty spot, placing the football down with precision. Then, forehead creased in concentration, she took a run-up and kicked the ball, hard. It soared into the top-right corner of the goal.

'Yes!' she cried, jumping up and down on the spot. Miss Kaur clapped in approval.

'Yeah, yeah, well done. Do you want a medal or are you going to move out of my way?' William snarled. He stepped up behind Mimi, looming over her.

Mimi narrowed her eyes, but she stepped aside, moving next to Leah. 'Let's hope his big head doesn't weigh him down and cause him to trip,' she muttered. Leah laughed.

William didn't trip. He took the penalty with a confidence that Leah couldn't help but envy. The ball soared effortlessly into the net, and William shot her a smug smile.

'Beat that,' he said. He strode past her, his shoulder smacking purposefully into hers and making her stumble.

'What a jerk,' Mimi muttered.

Leah tried to shake it off. She rolled back her shoulders as she stepped up to the mark. Above, the sky had grown very dark, and an ominous rumble reverberated around the field. As she stepped backwards, preparing to make her run-up, Leah's heart began to hammer in her chest. She stared at the goal and the great expanse of space around the goalkeeper. *She could do this.* There were plenty of places she could send the ball. In her mind, she imagined it darting through the keeper's outstretched hands and hitting the back of the net with a satisfying woosh.

'She's bottled it again.' William's rude shout cut her visualisation into ribbons. 'She can't do it!'

'Hush, William!' Miss Kaur's voice was angry. 'Come on, Leah! You've got this!'

But she didn't. The reality of the situation came crashing down on her all at once. Leah began to breathe faster and faster, the breath hissing through her teeth. William was right. The goal was too small. The goalkeeper was too fast. Leah's aim wasn't good enough. All the reasons why she couldn't take this penalty spiralled through her mind.

Suddenly, a fat droplet of water splashed onto her forehead. It was followed by another and another as the heavy, metal-grey clouds above released a torrent of cold, wet rain.

Miss Kaur blew her whistle and frantically began collecting up the footballs. 'Quick,' she shouted, beckoning them towards the changing room. 'Inside!' The team didn't need telling twice. Teeth chattering, everyone sprinted towards the benches.

Everyone but William.

He picked up his ball and threw it casually towards Leah, his mouth crooked into a malicious smile. 'Great penalty practice,' he said nastily. 'You're really gonna lead us to victory.' Then he turned and jogged after his teammates.

Clutching the football, Leah trudged miserably after him. She'd frozen. Again. In spite of what Miss Kaur had said. Disappointment and embarrassment surged through her. What kind of player couldn't take a penalty? And if she couldn't even do it successfully during training, what hope did she have of doing it in a proper match? What a complete disaster.

By the time Leah reached the changing room, most of the other players had left. Only Mimi and George lingered, waiting as Leah silently changed out of her wet kit and grabbed her coat. They headed to the school gates, securing their hoods and dashing out into the storm, past the shopping centre across the road and into the park. They slowed down as they neared the twisted oak tree at the centre. Its bare branches looked black against the gloomy mass of clouds overhead, like gnarled fingers outstretched to catch the ferocious raindrops.

'See you here at eight-thirty tomorrow morning?' George shouted over the roar of the rain.

Leah and Mimi nodded in agreement. Leah then opened her mouth to respond, but suddenly the hairs on her arms rose and a sharp crack ripped through the air as a light flashed. She blinked frantically, trying to clear the black spots that danced before her eyes. There was a slight ringing in her ears.

'What was that?' George gasped. He was hunkered down, his hands protectively clutching his camera, which he'd managed to zip underneath his coat.

Mimi lifted her arms up in front of her. 'I think it was lightning! The hairs on my arms stood up like soldiers! That's always a tell-tale sign. It's the electrical charge,' she shouted. Mimi always paid attention in science.

'It must have been really close. It could have hit us!' Leah exclaimed. All thoughts of football training had vanished from her mind.

'We should get inside, quick,' George said

nervously. Rain dripped from his nose and his teeth chattered.

'Good idea,' Mimi agreed. 'The next one could be even closer!'

Shuddering at the thought, they waved goodbye and, with one final look at the ominous silhouette of the oak tree, hurried away towards home.

CHAPTER 3:
THE POCKET WATCH

Leah found it impossible to sleep that night. Outside, the rain continued to pour down and battered against the house. She squeezed her eyes shut, but her thoughts rushed about noisily in her head. She couldn't stop them. William Riley's smug face danced tauntingly behind her eyelids. Even when she managed not to think about him, the big match against Westfield High on Thursday loomed in her mind. Plus, there was an important history test scheduled for the next day and she hadn't even thought about opening her textbook to revise.

Leah sighed noisily and shook her head, trying to dislodge the troublesome thoughts from her mind. When she finally did fall asleep, her dreams were full of empty penalty spots and a deep thunder that seemed to shake everything.

The blaring of her alarm woke her. She rolled over with a groan, slapping a hand over the clock and hauling herself up. She rubbed her eyes and yawned. Outside, blue skies sparkled and sunlight poured into her bedroom. Leah grinned. The storm was gone!

'Leah!' her mum called. 'Hurry up, or you're going to be late for school!'

Leah just had enough time to scoff down a piece of toast before she scooped up her backpack from where she'd left it at the bottom of the stairs the night before. She shouted goodbye to her mum as she set off, slamming the door behind her.

The morning was bright and perfect; you never would have guessed that a vicious storm had wracked the town just hours before. The only thing that gave it away were the numerous puddles that Leah leapt over as she rushed to the oak tree, where she always met Mimi and George before school.

It didn't take her long to reach the park. Leah

slowed her steps as she took the meandering path that led to the tree at the centre of the green, admiring how pretty everything looked in the sunlight.

Suddenly Leah stopped, gasping in horror. *The tree!*

Where once the old oak tree had stood tall and proud, there was now nothing but a tangle of roots reaching up into the sky. The trunk lay across the path, its branches snapped and broken. Leah stepped over them delicately as she inched closer, her eyes wandering over the destruction.

Leah looked up to see Mimi and George hurrying towards her from the other side of the park. They gaped at the fallen oak.

'Look,' said Leah, pointing towards the trunk. A great crack split the middle, the pale wood inside exposed like the innards of a giant fruit. The edge of each side was black, as if it had been charred over a barbecue. 'I think it might have been hit by lightning.'

George snapped a photo. The little box-shaped camera whirred as it spat out a small square photo.

George plucked it out, staring at it impatiently while the picture developed.

Mimi shrugged. 'It could be, but I think that's probably more likely down to the wind. It was really strong last night.'

'That's so sad,' said George, sliding the photo into his pocket.

Mimi peered at the roots, poking at them with a fallen branch she'd picked up. Leah joined her. The underside of the tree looked like a map, each root a thin road criss-crossing over another.

Mimi had turned her attention to the unearthed soil beneath the tree. She stuck the branch into it and moved the mud to and fro.

'Hey!' George said. 'Smile and pretend to dig!'

The two girls beamed up at him, their makeshift spades raking through the soil as he raised his camera and took their photo. As he pressed the shutter, Leah's branch sank further into the dirt. There was a muffled *clunk* as it hit something solid.

'What was that?' Mimi exclaimed.

'I don't know,' Leah frowned. 'Quick, help me

move this mud!'

Using both their hands and the branches, Leah, George and Mimi burrowed through the soil until they could see a hint of something metallic and shiny peeking through. Leah dug her fingers around the corners and, after a couple of insistent tugs, the item reluctantly came free.

It was a plain silver box, locked with a small padlock. Leah tried to wipe off as much of the mud as possible, looking for any clues as to what it might be. But there was nothing.

'Maybe it's buried treasure,' Mimi suggested.

'Like pirate loot?' Leah raised her eyebrows.

'It could be a time capsule,' George suggested.

'It would be a very old capsule if someone had planted it underneath that massive tree,' Mimi said slowly. 'Can you open it, Leah?'

Leah shook her head. 'No. Look at the . . .' She broke off abruptly as she touched the padlock. She'd thought it was locked, but as soon as she touched it a tingle swept over her fingertips and it swung open. The trio exchanged a look. Carefully, Leah unhooked the padlock, prying the lid open slowly. She peered inside.

'What is it?' Mimi demanded, jostling Leah's shoulder. George had his camera raised, finger poised over the shutter button.

'It's a . . .' Leah frowned. 'It's a pocket watch.'

Leah reached in and scooped out the watch, and its thin chain unspooled beneath it. It was heavier than she'd thought it would be. Its silver casing winked in the sunlight. Delicate filigree patterns were etched into its curved body and Roman numerals ringed the edge of the white face that was encased beneath a panel of glass. Two black hands reached out from the centre, their pointy tips like tiny spears. Leah waited for them to move but they were motionless . . . She held the watch up to her ear, listening for the *tick-tock*, but it was silent.

'It's broken,' Leah said disappointedly.

'Wait!' George said. He took the box from Leah and stuck his hand in. 'There's something else!' It was a scrap of paper, yellow and crinkled.

'Is it a love letter?' Mimi cried excitedly.

George shook his head. 'It says, "For those who might need it most". That's it.' He scrunched up his nose and showed them the paper. Leah could see the words written in a faded, cursive script.

'Oh man,' Mimi moaned, rolling her eyes. 'We got all muddy for nothing.'

Leah peered at the watch. Who would bury a watch beneath a big old oak tree? It must have been there for years, waiting for someone to dig it up.

'What do you think it means? What kind of person would need a broken pocket watch?' she asked.

George shrugged. He leaned forward and took another quick picture. 'Whoever it is, I don't think it's us.'

'I hate to interrupt this episode of *Time Team*,' Mimi piped up, her phone in her hand. 'But this mystery is going to have to wait for another time.

If we don't get a move on, we're going to be late for school. I don't fancy getting on Mr Cook's bad side first thing in the morning.'

Mimi was right. If they didn't hurry, they'd be in trouble! Leah stuffed the metal box into her backpack. But for some reason she couldn't bear the thought of the watch rattling around in there, so as they dashed through the park, she slipped it into her trouser pocket, where it would be safe.

CHAPTER 4:
NOON OR NIGHT

Leah slid into her seat just as the morning bell rang. She itched to look at the watch once more, but she didn't want to risk any of the teachers seeing it. Instead, she stuck her hand into her pocket and ran her fingers over the engraved edges. Her form tutor had to call her name three times before she answered for the morning register.

Maths wasn't much better. Leah was only dimly aware of the numbers Miss Maloney was writing on the board. She couldn't stop thinking about the watch. It seemed a strange sort of thing for someone to bury beneath a tree. What use was a watch if it was hidden under piles and piles of mud *and* a massive oak? Besides, hadn't the watch's owner known that the tree would grow too big for anyone to be able to find it?

Leah shook her head. It didn't make any sense. If not for the storm, who knew how long it would have been hidden under all those roots.

Unable to resist, Leah slipped the watch from her pocket. The silver casing looked even shinier in the glow from the classroom's fluorescent lighting. She flipped it over in her hand, marvelling at how pretty it was.

Wait a minute . . . There were words on the back! In the rush to get to school, Leah hadn't noticed them. She frowned and brought the watch closer to her face. The letters were etched so finely that it was difficult to read them properly, but if she just tilted it a little bit . . .

'Two hands meet at noon or night . . .' she murmured to herself. 'Click once, click twice and set time right.' What on earth did that mean?

'Leah!'

Leah jumped, her hands automatically shoving the watch beneath the table and into her pocket. Heart thumping wildly, she looked up at Miss Maloney, who was staring at her with an irritated scowl on her face.

'S . . . sorry, Miss Maloney,' Leah stuttered. 'What did you say?'

Miss Maloney's frown grew even deeper, but now she looked concerned rather than angry. 'I asked if you could answer the question on the board.'

Leah bit her lip. She hadn't been concentrating at all. She fumbled her way through the sum, trying to ignore the excited buzzing in the back of her head. She couldn't wait to tell Mimi and George about what she'd found!

'What does *that* mean?' Mimi asked as they strode towards their history class. 'It sounds like gobbledygook to me.'

Leah shook her head, turning the watch over in her hands. 'I don't know, but I feel like there's something special about this watch. There are just too many things that don't add up.'

George looked dubious. 'Are you saying you think it's, like, magic or something?'

'No,' Leah said quickly, blushing a little. 'I

know that magic isn't real, George. I'm just saying it's strange, that's all.'

'Hey!' Mimi suddenly exclaimed, stopping in the middle of the hall. 'I think I've worked it out!'

'Worked what out?' George said, puzzled.

'The riddle!' Mimi grabbed their arms and pulled them to the side. '*Two hands meet at noon or night, click once, click twice and set time right!* The noon bit is obvious — that just means midday, right? But I bet the "night" bit is talking about *mid*night. They're the same thing — the hands meet at the twelve!'

'But . . . the watch is broken,' George replied slowly. 'The hands don't move.'

'Duh,' Mimi replied. 'But we can move them ourselves. That's what that little sticky out bit does.' She pointed towards the button-like dial at the top of the watch.

'I think it's called a crown,' George said.

Leah felt a fizz of excitement bubbling in the pit of her stomach. *Mimi was right!* Tentatively, Leah touched the crown, pushing it gently. She'd expected it to be stiff after having been buried beneath the ground for so long, but the small silver knob twisted easily. As it turned, the black hands on the clock face began to move too, inching from 'III' to 'IV'. Leah twisted it again and again until the spiked heads of both hands were pointing at the numeral XII.

'Okay, what now?' George asked, peering at the clock face in trepidation.

Leah shrugged. 'The inscription says we need to click once, click twice. The only thing I can see that looks like a button is the crown itself. So . . .' She looked up at her friends. George and Mimi huddled closer, leaning over the watch eagerly. Leah's hand hovered over the crown. She took a deep breath, squeezed her eyes shut, and pressed it twice.

Nothing happened.

'Oh,' George said, disappointed. 'It really is broken.'

Leah blew her breath out in one big rush. She'd known it was silly to expect that the watch might do something. It was just a clock, after all. But she'd been so sure there was more to it than two long-stopped hands. Why else would it have been buried? And with such a mysterious note, too! But it really *was* just an old, broken watch.

Abruptly, Leah felt a twist of anger. She could feel her cheeks burning. She shoved the watch into her pocket without looking at it.

'Well, at least we tried,' Mimi said, her lips pursed into a despondent pout.

'Move out of my way, losers!' Something barged into Leah's shoulder and Mimi lurched forward, stumbling over her feet. George just managed to catch her before she tipped over and landed square on her face.

'Hey!' Mimi shouted. 'Watch where you're going!'

A cruel laugh answered her and Leah looked up into the face of William Riley. As if things couldn't get any worse! He was flanked by his cronies, Katie MacIntyre and Toby Henderson. Toby was big and burly, like a bear, while Katie was as thin as a kebab skewer, with a long nose and a pointy, weaselly chin.

'Look who it is,' William sneered, his sunken

blue eyes bright. 'Our fearless leader. Ready for another training session, Leah?' His tone was taunting and Leah felt her face growing hot.

Mimi started forward, her mouth tight with fury, but Leah caught her arm. 'Don't, Mimi. He's not worth it.'

Katie and Toby snickered. Wearing a broad grin, William leaned forward. 'See, guys? She's too chicken to do anything. I don't know what Miss Kaur was thinking, choosing *her*.'

'I hate to interrupt this very important "meeting",' came an imperious voice from down the corridor. 'But, as surprising as this may be to you, I don't have all day to waste waiting for you lot to decide whether or not you'd like to attend your history lesson.'

Leah fought the urge to groan as she, Mimi and George turned towards the voice. It was Mr Cook. He was standing in the doorway to their history classroom, hands on his hips, his impressive eyebrows drawn into a disapproving frown.

William smiled angelically towards their

teacher. 'I was just telling these three that they needed to hurry if they didn't want to miss your lesson, Mr Cook.'

'It's a shame more students aren't as conscientious as you, William,' Mr Cook gave an approving nod.

The three of them followed William, Katie and Toby into the classroom. They murmured their apologies as they hurried past Mr Cook, cringing under his stare. Leah shook her head as she sat down, pushing both William's words and her thoughts about the pocket watch out of her mind. She wouldn't let William get to her, and she certainly wasn't going to fixate on a stupid old clock. As soon as school was finished, she'd put it back in the box and return it to the tree.

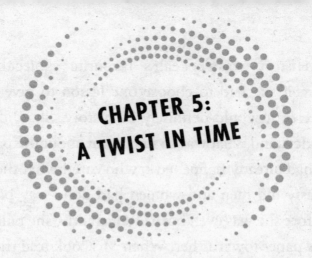

CHAPTER 5:
A TWIST IN TIME

Leah was already in a bad mood, so when Mr Cook announced that they were going to be taking a history test, her temper dipped from a stormy grey to an inky black. Mimi, who was sitting at the desk across the row with George, rolled her eyes and mimed hitting her head against the table. Leah's lips twitched.

'The results from this test will go towards your final grade at the end of the term,' Mr Cook was saying as he passed out the papers. 'This is a chance to really show me what you've learned this year.' He slammed the test down in front of Leah and gave her a meaningful look. It was almost like he was trying to inform her that he already knew she hadn't learned anything.

History wasn't Leah's favourite subject. In fact, if she had to choose one lesson to give up *forever*, it would definitely be history. She didn't understand what was so important about the past. It had already happened – who cared what those musty old men and women had done way back before she was even born? Reluctantly, she pulled the paper towards her. When Mr Cook told them to start, she flipped over the first page.

Her eyes scanned the first question, and she let out a sigh as she realised she had no idea how to answer it. First her disaster of a penalty practice, and now this. What a week! Resigned, she stared at the clock on the wall, urging the hands to move faster so she could just get out of there and go to lunch.

Suddenly, Leah's mouth dropped open. Lunch time! The bell went every day at midday or, as Mimi had pointed out, noon. *At noon or night . . .*

Maybe George was right and the watch really wasn't magical, but what if they'd just misunderstood the riddle? Leah believed that Mimi had worked it out correctly. The hands *did* need to be pointing towards twelve and the crown *was* the right button to click. But just because the hands were in the right position, that didn't mean that it really was twelve o'clock, did it? When Leah had moved the hands earlier, the time had been half past eleven. Maybe they needed to wait until it *actually* was noon!

Leah frantically tore a piece of paper off the corner of her test paper and scribbled a quick note. She folded it up and, after a furtive glance around to make sure no one was looking her way, she threw it across the row. It landed neatly in the middle of Mimi's test paper. Mimi started to unfold it, but she wasn't quick enough.

'Mr Cook!' William's voice rang out across the classroom. 'Leah's passing notes!'

Leah grimaced as Mr Cook's attention zeroed in on her. That little snake William. He'd been watching her this whole time!

Mr Cook strode towards her. Mimi and George scrambled to shove the note under the desk, but . . . it was too late. Mr Cook had already seen them.

'Well,' he said, his voice full of quiet fury. 'It's clear that none of you are taking this class seriously. If you want to waste your education, that's fine by me, but I won't have you in this classroom ruining everyone else's. You can wait outside for the remainder of the lesson. I'll see you once we're finished.' He pointed a quivering finger towards the door.

Leah, Mimi and George gathered their things, slinging their backpacks over their shoulders. As they left, Leah cast a glance over her shoulder. William Riley was grinning at her.

'My mum is going to kill me,' George said miserably once they were outside. 'If Mr Cook rings her, I'm going to be grounded for life.'

'I'm sorry, George,' Leah said. She was fumbling in her pocket for the watch. 'But we've got more important things to worry about!'

'Leah, we already tried,' Mimi said patiently as Leah brought out the watch. 'It didn't work.'

'Yeah, but it wasn't the right time – that's what my note said! What if we had to actually wait until the clock hit noon in real life?'

Mimi looked thoughtful for a second and then a wide grin spread across her face. 'You could be right!' she said excitedly. 'We should have considered all the variables earlier. What time is it now?'

George checked his phone. 'It's one minute to twelve,' he said. 'But guys, I really don't think it'll make a difference. There's no such thing as magical watches.'

'You don't know that,' Mimi said stubbornly. 'I watched a documentary once–'

'Let's look at the inscription again,' Leah interrupted, holding the pocket watch out in her palm. 'Just to make sure we haven't missed anything.'

The three of them leaned forward. Mimi raised a finger and stroked the delicate letters.

'We could just give it a go,' Leah said excitedly.

George gave a noisy, exasperated sigh. 'I can't believe we're still talking about this, but if you won't let it go . . .'

George extended one finger, and before Mimi or Leah could stop him, clicked the crown of the watch once and then twice, just as the school bell went off – its shrill scream signalling the end of lessons and the start of lunch.

Suddenly, everything seemed to slow. The ringing of the bell became long and deep, as if it was underwater. The doors along the corridor that had begun to open stopped – or at least they slowed down so much that Leah could barely see them moving. Then the corners of her vision began to blur, and the familiar surroundings of the corridor started to dissolve, swirling around and around like sugar being stirred into tea, until all Leah could see was a maelstrom of purple and blue. Her stomach flipped. Abruptly, she, George and Mimi were falling headfirst through a flashing tunnel of silver and gold. Leah's fingers were glued to the pocket watch and her ears popped unpleasantly. She heard Mimi scream and could see George's free hand clenched around his camera strap.

Leah tried to keep her eyes open, but the colours began to stream past her, moving faster and faster, until she had no choice but to squeeze her eyelids shut, surrendering to blissful darkness.

CHAPTER 6:
INTO THE PAST

Their landing wasn't graceful. Leah stumbled, her legs crumpling like paper. Her shins connected painfully with the floor, and she could feel small rocks digging into her knees. She heard the others crash to the ground with a shout on either side of her. She opened her eyes but it was hard to see – after travelling through that swirling tunnel of light, her eyes were all blurry.

George gasped. 'Where are we?' he cried. He sounded frightened.

Leah blinked hard, trying to get rid of the black, fly-like spots dancing before her eyes. When they eventually cleared, she peered around, taking in the scene before her. But she couldn't understand what she was seeing. She gave each eye a firm rub, but it made no difference. Nothing changed.

They weren't in the school corridor anymore. They were outside on a patch of grass. The sky above them was a watercolour of moody-looking clouds, each a different shade of grey. In front of them was a wide, squat building that looked like a cross between a posh manor and an ordinary house.

'Guys!' Mimi exclaimed. 'Look!'

She was pointing towards a white sign in front of the building. The three of them hurried towards it, eager to get a better look. In thick black letters were the words 'Crickle End Secondary School'.

'That's not our school!' George protested with a worried frown.

Leah was studying the building before her. George was right – this *definitely* wasn't their school – although there was something familiar about it. It was much smaller, but she'd seen those windows before. And the stone pillars on either side of the door . . .

'Yes, it is,' she said, not believing the words coming out of her mouth. 'That *is* our school, but it also isn't. What's going on?'

'The shopping centre is gone!'

Mimi had turned away from the school and was looking towards the shopping centre across the road. Or, at least, she was looking towards where the shopping centre *should* have been. Instead, the modern glass building had been replaced by something else. Leah gaped – it was the unmistakable structure of a football stadium. She could see the tin roofs arcing over the stands like giant bird wings, shielding the seats below. Directly in front of them there was a row of turnstiles. They were still and empty now, but she could almost picture the eager hands that would push through them before the start of a game.

'What's going on?' she whispered, looking around in bewilderment. With a jolt she realised she was still holding the pocket watch in her hand. Its chain dangled innocently through her fingers, and its metal casing was warm to the touch.

George followed her line of sight. 'No way!' he exclaimed. 'It can't have been the watch. Magic doesn't exist!'

'How else would you explain . . .' Leah paused, and then gestured at the football stadium and the strange school. 'This?'

'Well, it's obvious, isn't it?' announced Mimi, her hands on her hips. Her braids bounced

energetically around her face as she spoke.

'Is it?' George said dubiously. One hand was clenched tight around the camera straps hanging from his neck, while the other fiddled nervously with his glasses.

'Of course!' Mimi paused, dramatically. 'It's aliens!'

'Aliens?' Leah repeated.

'Yeah! We've *obviously* been abducted by aliens!'

'Mimi,' Leah shook her head. 'I'm not sure that's what happened—'

'No, listen,' Mimi interrupted. 'That watch is clearly an alien artefact. Some mysterious storm blows into town and we *coincidentally* discover this watch that catapults us through a freaky flashing tunnel to who knows where! I watched a documentary about a man who saw bright flickering lights and then the next thing he knew he was waking up in his back garden after an alien abduction. He had no idea how he got there!'

Leah screwed up her nose. Mimi was right, that tunnel had been full of freaky flashing lights, and they really didn't have any concrete idea about how they'd ended up here. But *aliens?* She wasn't so sure.

George raised his camera to his eyes and took a photo of the stadium. 'This is really weird.' He spun in a circle, taking everything in. Abruptly, he stopped. 'What are those people *wearing?*'

Leah followed his gaze. Figures scurried along the paths on either side of the road. There wasn't a pair of jeans or a hoodie in sight. All of the women were wearing shin-length dresses or skirts with puffy blouses and large flouncy collars. Their heads were topped by boxy hats, fake flowers and extravagant feathers protruding from the fabric folds. The men were dressed just as strangely. Suit jackets covered pale button-down shirts tucked neatly into long cotton trousers. Braces ran up their shirts like railway tracks. One man strolled by with a pipe hanging from the corner of his mouth, wispy trails of smoke puffing out of the wooden bowl at the end and threading around his immaculately curled moustache.

'Woah!' Mimi shouted. 'Look at that!' The car

that bumbled down the road was as unfamiliar to Leah as the strange outfits. It was boxy and square with two large circular headlights at the front like a pair of eyes. Next to her, George's camera snapped another photo.

'We've got to get back,' Leah said faintly, shaking her head. She thrust the pocket watch out to her friends. 'Quick, grab hold!'

George and Mimi did as they were told. The journey through the tunnel must have dislodged the watch's hands, because neither were pointing at twelve. Frantically, Leah wound them back into position. Then she clicked the crown twice.

Nothing happened.

Leah clicked again, and then a third time, just in case. It was no use.

'It won't work,' Mimi declared. 'It's not noon anymore, and it certainly isn't midnight. We're going to have to wait.'

Panic started to rise in Leah in an overwhelming tide. *Wait? How could they possibly wait?* Her mum would be worried sick when she didn't turn up at home!

'What are we going to do?' Leah gasped. 'We need to get back!'

'L, calm down,' Mimi said, placing her hand comfortingly on Leah's shoulder. 'We will get home, just not yet. After all, we've got to be back for the big match on Thursday. Right, George?'

George didn't look convinced, but he nodded anyway.

Leah took in a deep breath through her nose. Mimi was right. They couldn't force time to move any faster. They'd have to be patient.

'Right,' Leah said, trying to stop her voice from shaking. 'We need a plan. First, we should try to figure out exactly where we are.'

'Why don't we ask that woman?' George said, pointing across the road towards a woman standing in front of the stadium. 'Maybe she can help us?'

'Good idea, George,' said Leah decisively, trying to sound more confident than she felt. 'I'm sure she'll be able to help us.'

Together, they walked towards the football stadium. Leah shivered as a chilly wind whipped at their clothes. She wished she had a coat.

'I'd better get some photos of this,' George muttered, lifting his camera up to his eyes and pointing it towards the stadium. He nodded to himself in satisfaction. 'Might give us some clues about what's going on.'

As usual, Mimi had pulled ahead, but as they drew closer to the stadium Leah slowed down. Up close, the woman didn't look as friendly as she had from far away. She was wearing a strange outfit too – a white, collared shirt tucked into baggy shorts above thick knee-high socks. Her red hair was pulled up into plaits and pinned at the back of her head. She was glaring towards the stadium gates.

'Mimi,' Leah called. 'Wait a minute–'

But it was too late. Mimi was already stretching up to tap the woman on the shoulder. 'Excuse me, my name's Amelia, and these are my friends, Leah and George. We were just wondering if you could help us.'

The strange woman turned around, scowling. She looked them up and down, taking in their unfamiliar clothes and her frown deepened. 'What do you want?'

'This might sound odd, but we were hoping you could tell us where we are,' Leah said, before Mimi could jump in.

The woman scoffed. 'I don't have time for this!' she declared. She turned on her heel to stride away.

Sensing that they were losing their chance to get some answers, Leah shouted, 'Wait!'

The woman slowed reluctantly and turned to face them, an expression of annoyance twisting her delicate features. Leah looked at her in desperation. 'Please?'

The woman sighed. Leah thought she heard her mutter the word 'ridiculous', but she answered them anyway, speaking extremely slowly, as if she suspected they might not understand her. 'You're at Crickle End Stadium, of course.' She pointed towards a big sign that Leah hadn't seen. 'The former home of the Crickle End Champions, finest women's football team in the town.' She waved two tickets in the air and handed them to

George. 'Here. I won't be needing them anymore.'

'Are you a footballer?' Leah said excitedly. She'd been to a couple of women's matches with her dad back home but she'd never met a real-life footballer before! She bet this woman had never frozen on the penalty spot.

'I *was*,' the woman said, shaking her head. 'Top scorer on the team. But not anymore. Not now the government has banned all women's matches.'

'Leah . . .' George said. His eyes were glued to the tickets.

'Wait a minute, George,' said Leah distractedly. 'What do you mean, they've banned all women's matches?' she asked the woman eagerly.

'"*The game of football is quite unsuitable for females, and ought not to be encouraged.*" That's what they told us.' Two angry red splotches had appeared on the woman's cheeks.

'Leah!' George said again, more urgently.

'What?' Leah whirled round, exasperated.

'Look!' George waved a ticket before her face. Leah scanned the scrap of paper. The word

'CANCELLED' had been stamped across it in big red letters. 'Look at the date.'

Leah's eyes darted to the top corner of the ticket and she froze. There, typed neatly, was today's date. But it was the year next to it that made Leah's mouth drop open in shock. January 15th . . . *1921*.

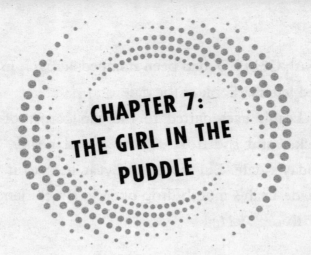

CHAPTER 7:
THE GIRL IN THE PUDDLE

Leah's mouth opened and shut like a broken kitchen cupboard. *1921*. It couldn't be true . . . could it? Had they . . . had they really travelled over *one hundred years* into the past?

'What is the matter with you three?' The footballer's voice was sharp with irritation. She shook her head angrily. 'I don't have time for this silliness!' She turned promptly and stomped away, her red hair like a fiery beacon against the greyness of the day.

Leah barely noticed. Her attention was focused completely on the four numbers in the corner of the ticket.

'Let me see that watch again,' Mimi demanded. When Leah turned to look at her, Mimi's mouth was pinched into a thin, anxious line. She fished the watch out of her pocket and handed it over, watching as Mimi flipped it and scrutinised the text on the back.

'Well,' she declared finally. 'It's obvious, isn't it?'

George rolled his eyes, 'That's the second time you've said that today! What's so obvious?'

Mimi held the watch up. 'This isn't an alien artefact. It's a time-travel device. Clicking that little crown has brought us back to 1921.'

George laughed. 'That's ridiculous.'

'Is it?' Mimi asked, raising an eyebrow. 'How do you explain all the weird clothes these people are wearing, then? And what about that funky car? Have you checked your phone? Have you got any signal?'

George spluttered, reaching for the phone in his back pocket. 'Of course, I do. Look . . .' he trailed off, dismay filling his face as he checked the screen. The signal indicator showed a flat line. Suddenly, his eyes looked very bright. 'Oh no,' he whispered, his free hand clutching at his camera. 'It's completely dead! What are we going to do? We're never going to get home!'

'Don't worry, George,' Leah reassured him, trying to ignore the queasy feeling in her stomach. She linked her arm through his. 'It's going to be okay. We won't be stuck here.'

'We won't?' George's bottom lip wobbled.

'No, we won't. The inscription says noon *or* night. Surely, if the pocket watch worked this afternoon, it'll work tonight too.'

Mimi suddenly grinned and hooked her arm around George's other elbow. 'Leah's right! All we need to do is wait until later and we can try again. We'll be home before you know it.'

'Although,' Leah observed, looking down at her blue hoodie, jeans and black trainers. 'We're going to need to do something about our clothes. We're going to stick out like sore thumbs otherwise. We need to blend in and act like we belong here.'

'Oh my goodness,' Mimi squeaked. 'Acting is my calling! This will be my first proper role!'

George laughed shakily, then pointed at the

pocket watch. 'I can keep that safe, if you want, Leah,' he offered.

'Thanks, George,' She handed it over and watched him slip it into his pocket.

Suddenly a loud, anguished cry pierced the air. Leah pivoted, scanning the front of the stadium for the source of the noise. Another shout echoed out again, this one tinged with anger.

'It's coming from round that corner!' shouted Mimi. She shot forward, sprinting around the side of the stadium and out of sight.

'Mimi!' Leah called after her. She grabbed George's hand. 'Come on, quick! Before we lose her for good!'

They ran in the direction that Mimi had gone, rounding the building containing the turnstiles. As they turned the corner, they heard a loud gasp and a splash. Cruel laughter echoed around them.

'What's wrong with you?' That was Mimi's voice. She sounded angry, and she looked it too. Her legs were planted wide, hands on her hips. At her side was an unfamiliar dog, its curly ears swaying as it yapped and barked.

Opposite was a group of children – two boys and two girls. The boys were dressed in knee-length shorts and matching jackets, and the girls were wearing loose dresses. Even though they looked nothing like him, there was something in their stances that reminded Leah unpleasantly of William Riley and his friends. They were all sniggering and pointing at something on the ground at Mimi's feet. Leah and George shuffled forward to get a better look.

It was a some*one* rather than a some*thing*. A girl, to be precise, about the same age as them. She was splayed on the muddy ground, her legs spread out awkwardly. It looked like someone had pushed her. Mud was smeared all over her checked smock dress, and dirty water stained the hem. Her once-white tights were now a grubby shade of beige.

As Leah and George watched, the girl pushed herself up. She pointed a quivering finger at the tallest boy. 'Give me that back!' she shouted. Her forehead was creased into a scowl, but her eyes were bright with tears.

The tall boy threw back his head and laughed nastily. 'Sorry, Dotty,' he sneered, his voice full of false sincerity. 'I can't. It's against the law for you to own something like this.' He placed his hand protectively over the football underneath his arm. At least, Leah thought it was a football. It was the right shape, but it was leathery, brown as a nut, and held together by thick black stitches. She'd never seen a football like it.

The girl clenched her hands by her side. 'That's not true!' she said through gritted teeth. 'It's mine. Give it back. Right now!'

But the girl's protests just made the other children laugh even harder. The tall boy leaned forward and patted her patronisingly on the head. She ducked away, hunching her shoulders protectively. 'I tell you what,' he said, puffing out his chest. 'I'm a generous person. I'll keep this football safe for you until they decide girls are *legally* allowed to play again.' The children around him dissolved into peals of laughter, and then, as one, they turned and sprinted away towards the road.

'No!' the girl shouted, causing the dog at Mimi's feet to let out a volley of barks. 'Come back!' She tried to dart forward, but the mud sucked at the heels of her shoes and she lost her balance. She fell back into the sludge.

'Oh no!' Leah gasped, and she, Mimi and George hurried to help her up. By the time the girl was steady on her feet, the bullies were already gone, taking the football with them. Dejected, she stamped her foot, sending little flecks of mud flying up into the air.

'Are you okay?' George asked, anxiously. 'Those kids were so mean!'

The girl shook her head. 'I can't believe they took my ball! My Pa bought that for me.' She heaved a great sigh. 'Thank you for your help, though. I really . . .' she stopped suddenly as she turned to face Leah, Mimi and George. Her frown deepened as she looked them up and down. 'What on *earth* are you wearing?'

Leah grimaced. They definitely weren't blending in.

'Are you part of the circus that's just pulled up outside town?' The girl asked, her eyes growing wide with excitement.

Before Leah could answer, Mimi stepped forward, throwing her hands into the air as if she'd just performed an acrobatic tumble. 'Yes!' she announced. 'We are. We're very adventurous circus performers, recently returned from an exotic tour of Europe.' Leah looked at George and they rolled their eyes.

'So . . . are you *clowns*?' the girl asked, confused.

'What?' Leah spluttered. 'No!'

'Do we look like clowns to you?' George demanded.

'Guys,' Mimi hissed. 'You're ruining my dramatic vibe!'

'Well,' the girl said, her tone imperious. 'You certainly don't look like you're from around here.' Her eyebrows lowered, and she suddenly looked very threatening. 'Who exactly are you?'

CHAPTER 8:
DOT

Leah stuck her hands on her hips. 'We should ask you the same question!' she said, tilting her head. She studied the girl in front of her. Her hair was the colour of coffee, cut into a bob that ended at her chin. Beneath brown, distrustful eyes, freckles dotted her nose.

'Are you an alien? Do you have a spaceship?' Mimi whispered.

'A what?' The girl looked confused. 'I'm Dot. I *live* here.'

'What, here?' asked George, pointing at the stadium.

'Not actually here, ninny. In Crickle End.' Dot frowned. 'Are you lost?'

'No!' Mimi burst out. 'We know exactly where

we are and exactly what we're doing.'

Dot looked sceptical. 'If that's true, why are your clothes so . . . peculiar?'

'*Peculiar?* My mum bought these trousers just last week – they're brand new!' George exclaimed.

'We're not lost,' Mimi insisted again.

Leah shook her head, exasperated. Despite her friends' best efforts, she suddenly realised that this wasn't going to work. They weren't fooling anyone. They looked too different and too strange. Dot had no reason to trust them. Of course, they had no way of knowing whether they could trust Dot either, but they had to trust *someone.* Leah didn't think they'd be able to blend in on their own. There was only one thing for it: she was going to have to tell the truth.

'We *are* lost,' she blurted out, interrupting Mimi's protests. 'We're actually very lost.'

'What are you doing, L?' Mimi hissed under her breath. Dot was watching them with interest.

'My name's Leah, and this is George and Mimi. And you're right,' Leah told her, 'we're not from this town. But it's more complicated than that.

We're not even from this *time*.'

'What do you mean?' Dot furrowed her brow.

Leah inhaled deeply. 'I mean, we're from . . . we're from the future.'

There was silence, then Dot gave a disbelieving snort that dissolved into loud chuckles. She laughed so hard that tears began to gather at the corners of her eyes. Leah, Mimi and George exchanged a bewildered look as Dot bent over and slapped a hand against her knee.

When she finally calmed down, her cheeks were a deep pink. 'The future?' she said, her voice strangled with laughter. 'Of course you're from the future. Do you have special machines that help you clean the house, like my Pa says there will be? Or how about streets that move you between places?'

'Well, there are vacuum cleaners,' George said.

'And travelators, but you only really get those at airports,' Mimi added.

'That's not important, though,' Leah interrupted. 'The important thing is that we're stuck here. We had this watch and we clicked it but now it won't take us home and we . . .' Leah trailed off as she realised that Dot wasn't listening. She was laughing again.

Leah's cheeks reddened. This was useless. 'Come on,' she muttered, turning to George and Mimi. 'This is a waste of time. She's not going to help us. We'll find someone else.'

'Wait, wait!' Dot wiped her eyes. 'I'm sorry. Look, you don't need to tell me where you're *really* from – I'll still help you.'

'You will?' asked George, sceptically.

Dot shrugged. 'It's the least I can do. I owe you a favour after what you did with those bullies.'

Leah sighed in relief, the tension finally leaking out of her shoulders. 'Thank you,' she said.

'I think I've got some dresses that should just about fit you,' Dot said, her eyes scanning Leah and Mimi. She nodded towards George. 'And my brothers will have something for you.'

'Won't they mind me borrowing their clothes?' George looked anxious, his fingers running nervously over his camera.

Dot shrugged. 'I've got four big brothers.

They won't even notice.' She suddenly frowned. 'Although, you won't be able to bring your dog into the house. My mum doesn't let us have pets.'

'What dog?' Leah asked, confused.

'That one!' Dot pointed to Mimi, and Leah suddenly realised that the strange dog she'd seen barking at the bullies was still there. He was sitting primly at Mimi's feet, tail wagging innocently as he looked up at them all.

'That's not our dog,' Leah said.

'He looks like a stray, actually,' Mimi added, bending down and ruffling his ears. 'He's a bit scruffy.'

Dot shrugged. 'Well, whoever he belongs to, he still won't be allowed in the house. Come on. The sooner we get you changed out of those . . . things, the better.'

Without waiting to see if they were following her, Dot marched away from the stadium.

'Do we go with her?' asked George uncertainly.

'We don't really have a choice,' answered Leah with a shrug, and she rushed to catch up with the mud-stained girl striding towards the road.

'Keep up!' Dot said over her shoulder. Leah noticed that the dog was trotting at their heels.

'How far is your house?' Mimi asked. George had his camera to his eye, capturing as much as he could.

Dot looked at him curiously. She seemed as if she were on the verge of asking exactly what his strange, black, boxy contraption was, but instead she just shook her head and said, 'Not far! But we'll need to be quick. I don't want my mum to come home and see you dressed like that!'

CHAPTER 9:
DISGUISES

It wasn't a long walk to Dot's house, but the route took them right through the centre of town. Back then, Crickle End wasn't a big place, but the streets were busy and bustling with people going about their business. As they hurried after Dot, Leah's eyes darted frantically from side to side, trying to take everything in.

She wasn't sure what she'd expected from 1921, but it was just as familiar as it was strange — she'd walked down these paths hundreds of times, but everything she knew was slightly different. The fried chicken shop her dad loved was gone, and in its place was a fancy opticians, which had a pair of fake, wire spectacles dangling over the door. The coffee shop wasn't there either; it had been replaced by a greengrocer's with a striped fabric canopy throwing its front into shade. Cars chugged up and down a thick strip of liquorice-black tarmac, and the familiar *put-put* of engines punctuated the burble of conversation echoing along the street.

But that was where the similarities ended. The boxy bodies of automobiles navigated the roads at a much slower pace, and they rattled more than Leah was used to. George gave a squeak as one driver hit his horn, the klaxon ripping through the air like a war cry – nothing like the smooth *beep* that Leah's mum's car made.

'Look!' George whispered. 'Horses!'

Leah turned to see a large cart pulled up at the kerb. The wooden bed was filled with coarse, brown sacks, lumpy with their cargo. Hitched to the front was the biggest horse she'd ever seen. Its coat was a deep, shining black, and it had a forelock of pure white dangling over its eyes. As they watched, it lifted one giant foot and stamped it down, the hoof making a loud *clop* against the tarmac. A boy seemed to appear out of nowhere, standing on tiptoes and running a comforting hand down the horse's long nose.

'Cool!' Leah whispered. George's camera spat out another picture.

'Hey,' Mimi said, tapping Leah on the shoulder. 'It's that dog. It's still following us.'

She pointed back the way they'd come and Leah twisted to see the small creature behind them, wagging its tail happily.

'I'm sure he'll lose interest when he realises we don't have any food on us,' Leah said.

'But don't you think he's pretty cute? I think he might be some kind of spaniel,' Mimi smiled faintly.

Leah groaned. Mimi loved dogs. No matter where they went, she always stopped to pet them, and she was always complaining about how her dad would *never* let her get one. Sometimes Leah and George had to forcibly drag her away.

'Don't get attached, Mimi,' Leah warned. 'We'll be going home soon, remember?' Mimi didn't seem to hear her, and with a roll of her eyes, Leah turned away.

Ahead of them, Dot was beckoning them forward impatiently. 'Faster!' she exclaimed. 'You're attracting too much attention.'

Dot was right. They *were* getting some rather strange looks, and Leah wasn't surprised.

'Everyone dresses like my grandparents,' George muttered under his breath. They picked up their pace, matching Dot's swift stride.

'Extra, extra! Read all about it!' As they rushed past a newspaper kiosk, the paper boy inside leaned out of the window and shook a paper in front of Leah's face. The picture on the front showed a group of women in football kits glaring unhappily into the camera.

'Hey, can I look at that, please?' Leah asked, pulling it from the boy's grip. Printed above the picture were the words 'Girls Given the Boot: Government Bans Women's Football'.

'That'll be tuppence, Miss.' The paper boy doffed his flat cap in the direction of the paper, and Leah didn't miss the strange look he gave her trousers.

'Uh, no thanks,' Leah passed it back to him.

Her fingers were smudgy with black ink, and she quickly rubbed them on her trousers as she jogged to catch up with the others.

'That paper says the government has banned women from playing football, just like that woman outside of the stadium told us.'

'Do you think that's why those kids stole Dot's ball?' asked George under his breath, so that Dot couldn't hear. 'They said it was against the law for her to have it and that they'd give it back when she was legally allowed to play again . . .'

'It must be,' said Leah.

'Poor Dot,' whispered Mimi, shaking her head. 'Imagine being told you aren't allowed to do something, just because you're a girl.'

'It's so unfair!' Leah growled fiercely. The thought of never being able to play football again made anger boil in her stomach. She knew she'd do whatever she could to get out on the pitch, even if it meant freezing on the penalty spot a hundred times over.

'Come *on*, you three!' Dot shouted back over her shoulder. 'Anyone would think you liked being the centre of attention!' She suddenly quickened her pace, breaking into a brisk jog, and disappeared down a side passage.

Leah, Mimi and George exchanged a look, then sprinted after her.

Dot's house was the middle one in a long row of red-bricked terraced houses. Tall and narrow, it reminded Leah of a library book, crammed into an overfull shelf. Dot led them up the path, but just before she opened the front door, she stopped.

'I told you,' she said, a touch impatiently. 'The dog can't come in here.'

Leah looked back towards the road. Mimi was crouched next to the small spaniel, running her hands over his fur.

'I've decided to call him Rolo,' Mimi piped up. Leah suppressed a groan.

'I don't care what his name is,' Dot answered. 'He's still going to have to wait outside.'

'Rolo, sit!' Mimi commanded. Rolo did as he was told, settling down onto his haunches. Mimi beamed at him and then at Dot. 'I think he'll be okay out here!'

Satisfied, Dot led them through the front door. It opened straight into a compact living room, two armchairs flanking a sooty fireplace like sentinels. A rickety-looking set of stairs wobbled their way up to a second floor, and there was a door set into the back wall. Leah craned her neck, trying to see through into the next room. She glimpsed a circular wooden table and a stove through the opening. The kitchen, she guessed.

Dot shut the door behind them with a bang

and gestured them up the stairs.

'How many brothers did you say you had, Dot?' Leah asked as they climbed.

'Four. And then me,' Dot replied as they emerged into a dingy, cramped landing with four doors. Dot went to the nearest one and opened it, ushering them inside. 'Because I'm the only girl, I get my own room,' she told them proudly.

Dot's room was pitch black. Leah stretched her arms out in front of her and her fingertips brushed what she thought was a wall.

There was a muffled bang. 'Ouch!' came George's voice.

'One moment!' A scratch, a hiss, and then a bloom of light. Dot had lit a candle, and its meagre flame gave the room a rosy glow.

Maybe the word 'room' was a bit generous; it was more like a large cupboard. There weren't any windows, and a single bed had been pushed up against the far wall. Pictures were stuck above it. Leah squinted, it looked like they were pictures of footballers, but it was so dark, she couldn't see properly. There was a narrow wardrobe to the side of the bed and a chest of drawers opposite. It was here that Dot jammed the candle into a holder.

'I usually have two or three candles in here, but we're running low,' she said apologetically. 'You can sit on the bed if you want.'

Leah and Mimi perched on the edge of the mattress, whilst George leaned against the drawers. Dot flung open the wardrobe doors and started rifling through hangers.

'These should do,' she said, grabbing three dresses similar to the muddy one she was wearing. She handed one to Leah and one to Mimi, keeping the third for herself. 'Try these boots on too.'

'George, come with me.' Dot grabbed his hand and pulled him out into the landing. 'We can steal some of my brothers' things. You look about the same size as Johnny.'

In the candlelight, Leah and Mimi changed out of their school uniforms and shrugged Dot's dresses over their shoulders. They were much thicker and scratchier than they looked, with a warm inner lining. Dot had left them some woollen tights too, and they pulled those on as well.

'I think these shoes might be too small for me.' Leah gritted her teeth as she tried to force her heel into the boot. Sighing, she gave up.

'Perfect for me, though!' Mimi said, her foot sliding neatly into the pair that Dot had given her. She laced them up tight to her ankles.

'That's better!' Dot exclaimed as she slipped

back into the room. She'd changed into a clean dress and tights. 'You look *normal* now.' She frowned as she took in Leah's bare feet. 'You'll have to wear your shoes until I can find you some that fit.'

Leah didn't mind. They might look strange with her dress and her tights, but at least her trainers were comfortable.

'Do I look okay?' George asked nervously. He sidled around the edge of the door and came to stand in the candlelight. He looked like the paper boy they'd passed on the street. He was wearing a beige shirt and loose brown breeches tucked into long socks. There were lace-up shoes, similar to Mimi's boots, on his feet. A brown flat cap made a valiant attempt to hold in his erratic brown curls.

'Wow, George! You look like you're about to star in a production of *Oliver Twist*!' Mimi exclaimed with a huge grin.

George blushed. 'You two look pretty funny too! Here, stand by the candle and I'll take your picture.' He raised the camera into position and clicked the shutter. The dimness of the room activated the flash, and it bleached the room bright white for a second.

'Ahh!' cried Dot, lifting her hands to her eyes. She blinked them frantically. 'What is that thing? It's burning my eyeballs!'

'Don't panic,' George reassured her. 'It'll fade in a moment.'

'It's just the flash overwhelming the retinas in your eyes,' Mimi told her matter-of-factly.

Dot scrubbed at her eyes, her nose screwed up. When she could finally see again, she glared at the camera menacingly. 'What kind of person carries around a torture machine that causes blindness?'

'This isn't a torture device!' George protested, offended. 'It's my camera!' He stroked the top of it reverently.

'A camera?' Dot scoffed. 'Yeah, right! I know what a camera looks like, and it's not *that*. Cameras are much bigger! You have to put them on a stand.'

George shook his head. 'Cameras aren't like that in the future. They're like this.'

'Uh, actually George, your camera is kind of

old-fashioned,' Leah pointed out.

'Not this future thing again!' Dot rolled her eyes.

'I promise it's true! Look, sit next to Leah and Mimi and I'll show you.' He moved a dubious-looking Dot into position between the two girls. Then he took their picture. Dot was more prepared this time, and once the flash faded she only had to blink her eyes a couple of times to clear them. The camera churned out the picture and George waited for it to develop before he showed it to Dot. 'See?'

Dot gasped. 'Oh my goodness!' She cried, grabbing the small rectangular picture and holding it closer to her eyes. 'It's magic!'

George laughed.

At the mention of magic, Leah suddenly remembered the pocket watch. For a second, panic filled her as she realised she wasn't sure where it was, but then she relaxed. Of course, she'd given it to George outside of the stadium.

'George, do you still have the watch?' She asked.

George patted his pocket. 'Right here. I moved it when I changed . . .'

'Good,' Leah said with relief. 'We're going to need it later. But now we're dressed properly, do you fancy showing us around the town, Dot? I'd love to see more of it!'

'Sure!' Dot hopped up from the bed, leading them out onto the landing. She shot down the stairs, with Leah, Mimi and George following at a more cautious pace. When they emerged into the living room, Dot was staring anxiously at a small clock on the mantelpiece over the fireplace.

'Oh no!' she shouted. 'We have to go!'

'What's wrong?' Leah asked in alarm as Dot yanked the door open.

'I'm late,' Dot sighed, frantically gesturing them out of the door. 'They said this was my final chance!'

CHAPTER 10: LOST PROPERTY

Dot led them down a side street at a quick trot.

'What are you late for?' Leah asked, jogging to keep up with her. Behind her, George and Mimi tried to match their pace, Rolo weaving between their legs.

'Laundry collection.' Dot's expression was grim.

'That doesn't seem so bad!'

Dot shook her head, biting her lip. 'Well, normally it's not. But this isn't *my* laundry. It's the football team's. And last time Mrs Matthews told me she'd throw it in the mud if I was late again!'

'Why are you collecting laundry for a football team?' Mimi asked curiously.

Dot threw a disbelieving look over her

shoulder. 'It's not just *any* football team. It's *the* football team. The Crickle End Champions!'

'We met one of their players,' Leah said, thinking back to the rude lady they'd spoken to outside of the stadium. 'She had red hair.'

'You met Mary?' Dot said. 'She's our best player! She's Mrs Matthews's daughter, too.'

'I'm confused,' Mimi said, frowning. 'Why are you collecting their kits if the government has banned women's football? They won't be able to wear them to any matches.'

'It's only banned *for now*,' Dot replied. 'Besides, the team will still need to train to keep their fitness up.'

'Are you on the team?' George asked.

Dot snorted. 'I *wish*. I'm not old enough yet. I'd love to be goalkeeper for the Champions one day, though. But I've got a long way to go until that's going to happen. I just help out where I can. Pick up their laundry, clean their boots, set up their training equipment. That sort of thing.'

'Like an internship?' Mimi said.

'Can we stop with the spaceships?'

'No, an internship is where you work for a company and do all the little jobs so that one day they might hire you to do the big jobs.'

Dot looked thoughtful, then she smiled and nodded. 'That's exactly it, then. An internship.' She rolled the unfamiliar word around in her mouth like a hard-boiled sweet.

'You know, me and Leah play football too,' Mimi told her.

'Do you?' Dot said excitedly.

'Yep! I'm pretty good, but Leah's the best player on our team. Right, L?' Mimi knocked Leah's elbow.

'Um, I'm pretty good, but I'm not the best . . .' Leah trailed off, her mind flashing to the disastrous penalty practice, the ball motionless at her feet as she stared into the goal.

'She's just being shy!' Mimi laughed.

When they finally stopped, it was outside a house that looked almost identical to Dot's. Even the front door was the same walnut brown. Dot hurried up the path and knocked on the door.

It opened almost immediately. A woman with

glasses perched on her nose peered down at them. Her hair was a faded chestnut, shot through with streaks of metal grey. Her round rosy cheeks and full lips should have made her look friendly, but her eyes were stern. Leah tried not to cringe as she swung those eyes to look at her. This must be Mrs Matthews.

'Dorothy,' Mrs Matthews's tone was short and clipped. 'What can I help you with?'

'Um . . . I'm here . . . um. The laundry.' Dot's tongue tripped over the words.

Mrs Matthews frowned and shook her head. 'No, no, you can't be. I distinctly remember that your laundry pick-up slot was much *earlier* than this!'

Dot's expression turned desperate. 'Oh please, Mrs Matthews! I'm sorry! It won't happen again.'

With a sigh, Mrs Matthews threw her hands in the air. 'I've heard that one before! Wait there.' She gave a disapproving *tut* and shut the door.

Dot gave a sigh of relief. 'Thank goodness. If I turned up without the kits . . .' she trailed off, her expression grave.

'I'm sure the team would understand,' Leah said.

'Maybe. But . . . ah . . . I have a bit of a reputation.' Dot looked sheepish.

'What do you mean?' Leah frowned.

Dot gave an awkward chuckle and shrugged. 'Let's just say this isn't the first time I've been a bit . . . disorganised.'

Leah opened her mouth to ask more but was interrupted by the *snick* of Mrs Matthews's door. She expected to see the laundress, but instead, a girl hovered in the doorway. She was a few years older than them, perhaps sixteen or seventeen, and her russet hair was braided into two plaits that hung over her shoulders. Her eyes were the same colour as maple syrup.

'Morning, Dot,' she said quietly. 'I thought I heard your voice.'

'Hi Anna,' Dot replied, smiling. 'I wondered if we'd see you here. These are my new friends, Leah, Mimi and George. They're from the circus.'

'Wow!' Anna smiled at them and Leah gave a small wave. 'That sounds very exciting.'

'Oh, it is!' Mimi piped up, but before she could say any more, Mrs Matthews reappeared in the doorway next to Anna. Unceremoniously, she leaned forward and dumped a white cotton sack into Dot's arms.

'I don't know why you won't just let my Anna deliver the kits, Dot,' she sighed.

Anna nodded in agreement. 'Mam's right. It's no trouble.'

'No!' Dot exclaimed, aghast. She took a deep breath and puffed up her chest. 'It's my responsibility.'

Mrs Matthews shook her head in despair but there was a faint smile on her lips. 'Well, you'd best get on with it. The team won't be impressed if you're any later.' Suddenly, she frowned, and Leah realised with a jolt that Mrs Matthews was looking at her. More specifically, she was looking at Leah's trainers.

Dot noticed too. 'Uh, you're absolutely right, Mrs Matthews. We shouldn't dally. Thank you. See you later at training, Anna!' Swiftly, Dot gripped Leah's arm and pulled her down the path, the laundry sack slung over her shoulder. George, Mimi and Rolo followed behind.

'Phew!' Dot exhaled, once the house was a little way behind them. 'I thought she was going to catch us out there! I just hope she doesn't tell my mother.'

'Anna seems nice,' Mimi said, as they took a left down an alleyway generously peppered with ferny weeds. 'Are you two friends?'

'Yep. Anna works for the team, like me. She's Mary's sister.'

'You seem to really like Mary,' Leah ventured.

Dot nodded vigorously. 'Of course! Everyone likes Mary. She's the best player on the team! Without her, there's no way we'd be top of our division.'

'She was pretty rude to us,' George muttered behind them.

'Does Anna want to be a footballer too?' Mimi asked.

'Of course she does. She applied to be part of the team last year, but she wasn't quite ready. She'll try again this year, though. After all, who doesn't want to play the greatest game in the world?' Dot said dreamily. They emerged from the alleyway back onto the Main Street they'd walked through earlier.

'I love playing football, but my feet are destined for the stage, not a muddy playing field,' Mimi declared loftily, flicking her chin up.

Dot's shoulders suddenly slumped, and she sighed. 'At this rate, my feet won't be doing any playing, either. Not with the news from the government.' She screwed up her nose and looked as though she might cry.

Leah suddenly felt very sorry for Dot. They weren't that different really; Dot had thought she had everything sorted and, just like that, everything had been tossed up in the air.

Leah placed her hand comfortingly on Dot's shoulder. 'Don't worry,' she said, trying to sound reassuring. She thought of the women's football matches she'd been to see with her dad. 'I'm sure you'll work it out. If you're meant to play football, you will. You'll find a way. They won't beat you!'

Dot stared at Leah, then she gave a decisive

nod. 'You're right,' she said, taking a deep breath and curling her hands into determined fists. 'I've got to believe. I won't let anything stand in my way!'

When they arrived at the stadium, George paused to snap a photo, but they didn't linger; Dot led them straight to the turnstiles and, one by one, they ducked beneath the still, silver bars.

The corridors of the stadium were quiet, and very dark. Rolo gave a whine.

'Ugh,' Mimi complained. 'Isn't there a light switch in here somewhere?'

'A what? Oh!' There was the sound of someone scrabbling, and then the familiar *click* of a switch. Light flooded the hall. 'That's better. We've only just had the eltricity installed here. I'm not used to it.'

'Electricity,' George corrected.

'That's what I said,' Dot answered. She took the lead again, trooping down the corridor. The others followed her as she turned right into a changing room. She flicked another switch, and a single lightbulb overhead flickered to life. Dot shook her head. 'I don't think I'll ever get used to it. Give me a good candle any day.'

'What are we doing here, Dot?' Leah asked curiously.

'This is where we're going to get you some normal shoes,' Dot replied. She dumped the bag of laundered kits on one of the benches and marched over to a door in the far wall. When she swung open the door, Leah could see at least six shelves, all lined with white canvas trainers. Dot began to hunt through them, before finally pulling a pair free. 'These should be about the right size!'

Leah sat on one of the benches and toed her trainers off, swapping them out for the ones Dot had given her. They reminded her of the plimsolls they used to wear in PE at primary school. They were a perfect fit, and surprisingly comfortable. Flexing her toes, she stashed her own trainers in her backpack.

'What now?' asked Mimi.

'I need to get these kits to the team,' Dot said. 'Before I'm really late!'

'Uh, Dot . . .' George sounded uncertain.

'What?'

'Where did you put the kits again?'

Dot turned towards the door. 'Just on that b—' She gasped, her hands flying to her mouth.

The bench was empty. The kits were gone!

CHAPTER 11:
THE THEFT

Dot darted around the changing room, crouching to check under the benches by the door. Rolo chased after her, as though it were a game.

'Oh no, oh no, oh no,' Dot groaned. 'This is bad, very bad.'

'Did you definitely bring them in with you?' Mimi asked, scanning the room.

'I did! I'm sure I did!'

Leah nodded. 'I saw her put them right there.'

With an anguished cry, Dot sank onto the very empty bench, her head dropping like a stone into her hands.

Mimi sat next to her, putting an arm around her shoulders. 'It's okay, Dot,' she reassured her. 'It's only a few kits. Surely the team can just use some others whilst we find the lost ones.'

Dot lifted her head. Although she wasn't crying, her chocolate-coloured eyes were red-rimmed. 'No,' she croaked. 'You don't understand. The kits in that bag were the *first* kits.'

'What do you mean?' Leah asked.

Dot sniffed. 'Back when the team first started out, the girls couldn't afford to have their kits made because the government wouldn't give them any money. So everyone brought in one of their own shirts, and then each personally stitched their own name and number onto the back. They've never lost a game whilst wearing them. It doesn't matter that the government has banned women's matches – they're special! They're lucky!'

'Oh.' Leah bit her lip.

'So, there aren't any spares?' Mimi asked.

'There are . . . but they're all blank.' Dot shook her head, squeezing her eyes shut. 'Oh goodness, the team are going to *hate* me!'

'Look,' Mimi stood up, pulling Dot up with her. 'The kits can't have just vanished – they must be here somewhere! Maybe you accidentally dropped them outside.'

Dot looked unconvinced.

'Yeah!' George piped up. 'We can go and see, at least.'

The four of them gave the changing room a last look before they moved out into the corridor, Rolo sniffing alongside them. They made their way out to the turnstiles and then to front of the stadium, scanning the floor. There was no sign of the kit bag anywhere.

'I told you!' Dot crowed, forlorn. 'They're gone! Someone's stolen them.'

'Why would anyone want to steal football kits?' Mimi said dubiously.

'I don't know but – *oh*!' Dot's voice cut off as Leah suddenly bumped into someone. She stumbled back, losing her balance and thumping down onto her bottom, her mouth an 'o' of surprise.

Looming over her was a tall, thin reed of a man. An inky-black suit jacket hung off his coat-hanger shoulders, and he was carrying a large blue sports bag in one hand. He sneered down at Dot, then transferred his pale blue glare to Leah, Mimi and George. A pair of wire spectacles perched precariously on the tip of his crooked, z-shaped nose. Rolo gave a low, threatening growl.

Mimi bent down to help Leah up as the man sniffed in disapproval. His voice slithered out like grease as he hissed, 'You should watch where you're going.'

'Sorry,' Leah apologised. 'I didn't see you.'

Her words only seemed to displease him further. He leaned forward and squinted at her, his lip curling. 'You should be at home, helping your mother, instead of careering around like a hooligan, bashing into

important people. Stupid girl.'

Mimi gasped, but before any of them could think of an appropriate reply the man had turned, his long legs striding confidently away from them.

'That was rude!' Mimi said, indignantly.

Leah brushed the dirt from her dress. 'Do you know who he is, Dot?' she asked.

'That was Mr Smelting,' Dot looked grim. 'He works for the government. I saw him at the training pitch yesterday when he came to tell the team about the ban. He's here to make sure the team follows the rules. He must have been hanging around to check the match really was cancelled.'

'I don't like him,' George said, and Leah nodded her agreement.

Mimi looked thoughtful. 'Did you see that big blue bag he was carrying?' she asked. 'A strange thing to carry when you're wearing a suit. Most businesspeople have briefcases.'

Dot gave a sudden gasp. 'Maybe *he* stole the kits! They could have been in that bag!'

George looked sceptical. 'Are you sure you're not jumping to conclusions?' He'd taken a stack of photos from his pocket and was absently flicking through them as they spoke.

Leah shook her head. 'No, Dot has a point! The match was supposed to be ages ago. What reason could Mr Smelting have to hang around here this late? He's got a motive too. If the kits are missing, the team *definitely* won't be able to play.'

'Actually,' George said slowly. He was staring down at one of his photos, 'you could be right. Look at this!' He held out the small square and the girls crowded in, craning over the picture.

It showed the stadium, but the area outside was mostly empty. Leah, Mimi and Dot were seen striding towards the turnstiles, and a couple of passers-by were strolling along the path. But in the left corner . . .

'There! It's Mr Smelting!' Mimi gasped, pointing. She was right. His stick-like stature leaning against the side of the stadium was easily recognisable, especially with the bright-blue bag slumped by his feet. 'This is proof. He must have taken the kits!'

Dot gave a groan and shook her head. 'What am I going to do? There's no way I'll be able to get them back now.'

'It's not your fault,' Leah tried to console her. 'The team will understand.'

Dot shook her head. 'I don't think it's going to be that simple. This isn't the first . . . incident.'

Leah tipped her head to the side. 'What do you mean?'

Dot bit her lip. 'Well, you know I told you earlier that I'm not the most organised? It's more than that. I'm a bit of a scatterbrain. They think I'm "unreliable". Once, I got the days of the matches mixed up, and there was that other time when the team asked me to look after the tickets for a game but I lost them all and . . .' she trailed off miserably. 'This will be the final straw. They'll never let me onto the team now.' Her eyes were bright as tears gathered in the corners.

Leah took her hand, squeezing it. 'Don't cry, Dot. You helped us, and now we'll help you. We'll get those football kits back!'

'But how?' Dot wailed.

Leah exchanged a determined look with George and Mimi. 'There's only one thing for it. We need to follow Mr Smelting and figure out where he's planning to stash them.'

CHAPTER 12: ESPIONAGE

'Just for the record,' George hissed. 'I think this is a really bad idea.'

Mimi sighed and shook her head in exasperation. 'We know, George. We heard you the first five times you said it.'

'Well, when this all goes wrong, I want to be able to say I told you so.'

It hadn't been difficult to catch up to Mr Smelting. Even if he wasn't carrying a bright-blue bag, he was so tall that his hat-topped head was clearly visible above the pedestrians on the path. Leah had motioned them to stay back, out of sight, so they were following him from a generous distance. He'd led them on a meandering route through the town, zigzagging across streets and dipping down alleyways.

'Where is he going?' Leah muttered as he turned down a particularly narrow lane that was pockmarked with puddle-filled holes and crammed with metal dustbins. She beckoned the others forward to follow him, her finger pressed to her lips and her shoulders tight with anticipation.

'You've got to be really quiet, Rolo,' Mimi whispered to the spaniel ambling at her feet. 'Mr Smelting can't know we're here.' Rolo panted and wagged his tail.

Cautiously, the group crept down the alley, dodging around dustbins. They were halfway down and Leah had just begun to relax when there came a sudden *clang!* Rolo's joyful tail had bounded off the side of one of the bins and the resounding *bong* rolled around the alley like thunder. With a sharp intake of breath, Leah ducked back behind a dustbin, pushing the others behind her, and Mimi snatched up Rolo out of sight. Mr Smelting stopped abruptly, turning his head to scan the space behind him. Leah squeezed her eyes shut – she felt sure that he'd spotted them. There was a beat of silence, during which they all held their breath. Mimi clutched Rolo to her chest. Then, with a sneer, Mr Smelting shook his head and continued on his way, his pace just as unhurried as before. Leah let out a sigh of relief. Once she was sure it was safe, she gestured to the others to come out of their hiding place.

'Where is he?' George asked, peering over Leah's shoulder as they emerged out into the street.

It took Leah a moment before she spotted Mr Smelting's tall form. 'There he is, over at that bus stop.'

'That's not a bus stop!' Dot said. 'That's for trams!'

Now that she'd said it, Leah suddenly noticed the railway-like tracks running along the road in front of her.

'Trams?' she said. 'We don't have any trams in Crickle End.'

As she spoke, a bell suddenly rang out, and there was a squeal as a tram rounded the corner.

It had two decks and its blue body gleamed as it chugged past. It reminded Leah of a cross between a boat and a bus.

'Wow,' George said, taking a photo. 'I've never seen a tram before.'

The tram pulled up to the stop and a wave of passengers flooded out onto the street. Amongst them all, Leah spotted Mr Smelting. He was getting onto the tram!

'Oh no!' she cried, pointing. 'He's getting away!' She started to dash forward, determined not to freeze like she'd done during training, but Dot's hand clamped around her arm, pulling her back.

'We can't follow him,' she said, her expression grim. 'We'll have to pay the tram fare and I don't have any money. Do you?'

Leah, Mimi and George exchanged a helpless look. Leah shook her head reluctantly. 'No, but we can't just let him get away with the kits!'

Dot grinned. 'We're not going to. I've got a backup plan.'

★

'Dot, how many times have I told you not to bother me when I'm with my friends?'

'I'm sorry, Charlie, but I really do need your help!' Dot peered up at her older brother, her eyes wide and pleading.

After they'd lost Mr Smelting, Dot had led them through a warren of streets until they'd arrived at an old, abandoned factory, its broken windows leering ominously over the street. Dot had explained that, back in the war, it had been one of the buildings used to make aeroplane parts. Dot had confidently led them through a broken doorway and into a large, dusty room where five teenagers were lounging, including her older brother.

Charlie looked just like Dot, but his hair was a shade lighter and he was much taller. He stared down at her through narrowed eyes while she spoke, then suddenly he gave a sigh, throwing his hands up into the air. 'Fine, but you'd better make it quick! What do you want?'

Dot took a deep breath. 'I need your map.'

Charlie's response was immediate. 'No way,'

he said, shaking his head. 'Not a chance.'

'Please, Charlie! I promise I'll be really careful.'

'That map is one of a kind!' he said. He transferred his suspicious glare to Leah, Mimi, George and Rolo. 'I don't want no circus kids getting their hands on it.'

On the way to the factory, the group had decided that they'd stick with their original story and tell Charlie they were part of the circus. Leah didn't want anyone else knowing where they were from, and seeing as how Dot didn't really believe them anyway, pretending to be circus kids was the easiest option.

'It's not for us!' Mimi protested. 'It's for Dot!'

'And the football team,' Dot added. 'Look, I'll do your chores for a whole week if you let me borrow it.'

Charlie snorted. 'A week? That's nothing!'

'Fine!' Dot said, desperately. 'A month!'

Charlie was silent, staring down at her. 'Chores for a month *and* your share of pudding on Sundays.'

'What?' Dot exploded. 'That's the worst deal

I ever heard!'

Charlie shrugged, folding his arms over his chest. 'It's that or no map, Dotty.'

Dot looked like she might argue further, but in the end she just gave a big sigh. 'Fine! It's a deal.'

Charlie gave a smile that said he knew he'd got the better end of the bargain. He opened his jacket and fished around in the inside pocket until he produced a folded-up piece of paper. Dot reached out to take it, but Charlie lifted it above his head. His expression was serious.

'No matter how much pudding you give me, I'm putting a lot of trust in you,' he said solemnly. 'You need to take special care of this map, Dot.'

Dot nodded enthusiastically. 'I promise, Charlie, I really do.'

Charlie waited a beat longer and then, satisfied, he handed over the paper. 'Now scram, squirt. You're embarrassing me in front of my pals.'

He watched them as they went back the way they'd come. Dot clutched the paper reverently to her chest.

When they got outside, George came to a stop.

'What is that, Dot? And how is it going to help us find Mr Smelting? You didn't really explain it before.'

Dot flashed a smug smile. 'When he was younger, Charlie wanted to be an explorer. He set himself a challenge to explore the whole of Crickle End and create a map.' She held up the paper square. 'This is that map. He's still adding to it, even now. It's the key to finding Mr Smelting.'

Leah, Mimi and George huddled closer as Dot began to unfold the paper. Leah gasped in amazement.

It was the most intricate hand-drawn map she'd ever seen. Each road had its name inked neatly down the middle and a small key in the corner designated the parks and local facilities. On top of all that, Charlie had added his own notes. In the corner, an arrow pointed to the best blackberry thicket to pick fruit for jam. Another showed a gap in a fence where you could sneak through into the cricket ground. It was very impressive.

'There!' Dot said, pointing. Whilst Leah had

been admiring the map, Dot had been searching for Mr Smelting's government building. 'It's not too far from here. We could go right now!'

'Hold on a minute,' Leah said. 'We can't just go charging over there, Dot. What if he's in his office? There's no way we could sneak in.'

George nodded in agreement. 'We should wait until we know he definitely isn't there.'

'Now we have the map, we can go whenever we like,' Mimi added.

Dot looked like she might argue, but then she closed her eyes and groaned. 'Oh dear,' she muttered, shaking her head.

'What?'

'It's just . . . if we don't go to the office today, that means I'm going to have to tell the team I've lost the kits. I was hoping we might be able to get them back and they'd never have to know.' Dot looked miserable.

'Sorry,' Leah said regretfully. 'It's just too risky for us to try anything now.'

'I know,' Dot said glumly.

'And it hasn't been a complete waste of time,'

Mimi said brightly, trying to sound cheerful. 'At least we know where Mr Smelting might have taken the kits.'

Just then, the sonorous *gong* of a church bell rolled out across the town. It sounded four times, signalling that it had reached four o'clock. The winter sky was fading from a stony grey to a dusky blue.

'The team will be gathering at the training field now,' Dot said reluctantly. 'There's no point in putting it off. I should go and tell them what's happened.'

'We'll come with you,' George offered. 'We were there too. We'll make sure they know it's not your fault.' Leah and Mimi nodded in agreement.

Dot looked grateful. 'Thank you. I don't know if it'll help, but I appreciate it anyway.' She cast one last longing look at the map and then sighed. 'Let's go. It'll only be worse if I'm late.'

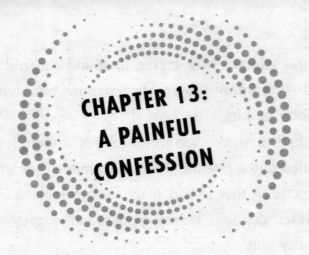

CHAPTER 13: A PAINFUL CONFESSION

Despite Dot's reluctant steps, it didn't take them long to reach the team's training ground. Located on the opposite side of town to the stadium, it was little more than a field, muddy in places from the winter rain. Leah could just see the vague shape of a football pitch marked on the grass, but the lines were old, the white paint flaking away. In the future, she vaguely recalled playing on a field just like this as a little girl, but it had eventually been turned into a new housing development. She wondered if this was the same field. To the left was a small wooden shack. It looked no bigger than their history classroom at school. Honey-coloured light spilled through the windows, inviting against the twilight gloom.

It was towards this structure that Dot led them. At the door, though, she paused. Her fingers hovered above the handle, and Leah could see that they were shaking slightly. She placed a comforting hand on Dot's shoulder.

'Don't worry,' she said. 'Whatever happens, we'll be right behind you.'

Dot gave a tremulous smile and nodded. She opened the door and gestured for Leah, Mimi and George to follow her inside. Rolo hopped in after them.

Leah wasn't sure what she'd expected from a professional football training session, but it wasn't the cacophony of raised voices and angry shouts that greeted them. Even Dot cringed at the uproar. The team were scattered around the room, some leaning against the grubby, peeling walls, and others slumped on the benches lining them. Leah spotted Anna huddled in a corner. No one was smiling.

'Are they always like this?' Leah asked, leaning close to Dot's ear to be heard over the noise.

Dot's face was grave. 'Never.'

There was a sudden bang as a fierce wind slammed the shack door shut behind them. Leah swallowed thickly as the arguments suddenly died and a dozen pairs of angry eyes swivelled in their direction.

'Yikes,' George muttered, clutching the strap of his camera.

'Dot,' said a woman standing at the front of the room. A mass of black curls surrounded her pale face, the erratic spirals bouncing in front of large, dark eyes. Her hands were braced against a table and there was a chalkboard on the wall behind her. It was covered in curving lines, and Leah thought they looked similar to the team tactics Miss Kaur often scribbled on the whiteboard. 'Where have you been? You're late.'

'That's hardly a surprise,' muttered a red-haired woman standing to the side. Leah recognised her as the rude lady they'd asked for help outside the stadium.

Dot's cheeks flushed crimson, but she ignored the comment. 'Sorry, Edie,' she said, addressing the lady by the table. 'I got caught up helping some friends. This is Leah, George and Mimi. They've just come into town with the circus. Guys, this is Edie Partridge. She's the captain of the Crickle End Champions.'

'For goodness' sake,' snapped the redhead. If she recognised them from before, she gave no sign of it. 'We don't have time to babysit circus brats, Dot. Don't you know what's been going on around here? All of our matches have been cancelled. *Cancelled!*'

'Mary, you don't need to shout at her,' Edie interrupted sharply. Mary glared at her, but Edie wasn't looking. Her attention was on Dot, her expression bemused. 'But we have got a lot to sort out, Dot. Why exactly have you brought them here?'

Tutting, Mary tossed her head back. A small 'v' pinched the skin between her eyes into a dismissive frown. 'What a waste of time,' she muttered sulkily.

Edie ignored her. Instead, she stared at Dot curiously.

'I'm not trying to waste your time, Mary,'

Dot said earnestly.

Leah remembered the way Dot had spoken about the woman on the way from Mrs Matthews's house. Dot had told her she was the best player on the team. Leah also suspected, from the expression that came over Dot's face when she talked about her, that she might be Dot's own personal favourite. 'But something has happened, and Leah, Mimi and George are my only witnesses.'

'What's happened?' Edie asked, her frown deepening. Leah felt a little sorry for her. What with the government ban, she was probably trying to juggle lots of different balls. No wonder Dot had been so reluctant to tell her about the kits.

Dot swallowed audibly. 'Well, you must promise not to be mad . . .'

The room filled with groans and sighs. Leah heard someone mutter, 'Not again!'.

'Dot,' Mary's voice was dangerously low. 'What have you done?'

Suddenly, Dot's courage snapped. 'It wasn't

my fault!' she wailed, burying her hands into her hair. 'One minute they were there, and then when I turned around . . . and I swear I didn't just *leave* them like that other time – Leah saw me . . .' Dot trailed off helplessly, aware that all eyes were now focused solely on her.

'Dot,' Edie's voice was resigned, but her eyes were kind. 'It's okay, but you must tell us what you're talking about.'

Miserably, Dot looked at her shoes. 'It's the kits,' she said wretchedly. 'The lucky kits are missing.' A cry of dismay went up throughout the room.

'Well, actually,' Mimi piped up before any of the team could say anything. 'They're not just missing. They were stolen.'

Mary gave a derisive snort and crossed her arms over her chest. 'Who would possibly want to steal a set of women's football kits?'

'It's true!' Dot protested, stepping forward. 'I picked them up from your house, Mary, and then we went to the stadium. I put them down on the bench in the changing room, and then when we turned round, they were gone!'

'What were you doing at the stadium?' Mary asked, her eyes narrowed in suspicion.

Leah blushed, thinking of the plimsolls on her feet. For the first time it occurred to her that they never would have needed to go into that changing room if Dot's shoes had fitted her.

Thankfully, Edie saved Dot from having

to invent an excuse for their changing-room excursion. 'Did you see anyone at the stadium? Anyone who could have taken them?' she asked.

'Yes!' Dot burst out, triumphant. 'It was Mr Smelting!'

'Smelting?' Mary repeated, but her voice had lost its sharp edge. Instead, she merely sounded thoughtful.

Edie, however, had fixed stern eyes on Dot. 'That is a very serious accusation to make, Dot.'

'It would make sense, Edie,' Mary spoke over the captain. 'Smelting knows what those kits mean to us. What better way to make sure we can't play?' Around the changing room, some of the other players were nodding in agreement.

'We ran into him outside the stadium,' Dot spluttered. 'He said some really unkind things to us.'

'And he had a big blue bag,' Mimi supplied. 'We think he grabbed the kits when we weren't looking and stashed them in there.'

Edie was quiet for a moment. Leah could almost see the thoughts ticking away behind her dark eyes. Finally, she heaved a sigh and shook her head. 'I'm not saying I don't think you're telling the truth, but I can't just go around throwing accusations at government officials. I'm not even sure they'd believe a women's football team over Mr Smelting, but either way, it would get us into serious trouble if you're wrong.'

Mary threw her hands up in exasperation. 'As if we're not in enough trouble already.'

'Look,' Edie raised her voice, addressing the rest of the players. 'I know how you feel about the kits. I feel it too! But it doesn't matter that they're missing if we don't even have a match to wear them for in the first place. Right now, we need to decide what our next move is. We can deal with the kits later.'

One by one the players nodded. The room gradually began to fill with noise again as the women resumed their conversations.

Leah leaned towards Dot. 'The match that was cancelled today, was it important?'

Dot stared as if Leah had just said something very stupid. 'It was the final of the Women's

Championship Cup.' She paused dramatically, her eyes going wide. 'It was the biggest match of the *entire* season. You should see the size of the trophy.'

Leah winced. It was bad enough that the team had been banned from playing at all, let alone just before the biggest and most important match of their year. Her thoughts drifted to her own football team and the game that awaited them on Thursday. She had to get home in time to play it.

Leah gulped, letting in the worry that she'd been holding at bay since they'd arrived. The watch would take them home, wouldn't it? They wouldn't get stuck here, would they?

She was suddenly snapped out of her thoughts by a loud voice. 'What else is there to discuss?' a woman with wavy blonde hair was saying. 'Everyone knows about the ban now, and the officials are all over us!'

'We've still got to play the final, though, Sarah,' another player replied. 'We can't just give up.'

'Why don't we just sneak into the stadium and set it up right under their noses?' someone else suggested, but Edie was already shaking her head.

'As much as I love that idea, Lizzie, they'll catch us for sure.'

Leah bit her lip, listening vaguely as the players volunteered different solutions, all of which were dismissed, one by one. A small kernel of an idea had started to grow in the back of her mind; if she could just get the players to listen to her . . .

But the thought of speaking up in front of all these people made her stomach wriggle like it was full of tiny worms. The last time she'd tried to take control of a situation had been that disastrous training session. Her mind conjured up the memory of William Riley insulting her in front of the whole team, his face glowing with satisfaction as she froze on the penalty spot.

No, this wasn't the same. These were grown-ups. They wouldn't treat her like that, would they? Especially not if the idea really was a good one that might help them.

Clenching her fists in determination, Leah cleared her throat. No one so much as glanced her way, except for Mimi, George and Dot, who all gave her a strange look.

'Are you getting a cough, L?' George asked, concerned.

'No! I just . . . I'm trying to . . .' Leah huffed in frustration. If this was going to work, she had to be louder and she had to be confident. Like Miss Kaur. She always knew how to get the team's attention. Puffing up her chest, she took a deep breath and said loudly, 'Excuse me, but I think I have an idea.'

Her voice filled the whole room. It was like she'd spoken into a megaphone. *She'd done it!*

Leah was so elated at her success that it took her a moment to notice that the room was completely silent. She gulped as she suddenly realised that everyone was looking at her, their conversations cut off mid-sentence.

'What are you doing, L?' Mimi hissed.

'Who are you again?' Mary said, her small nose wrinkled in annoyance.

'I'm . . . I'm . . .' Leah took a deep breath, trying to get her hammering heartbeat under control. *Confident*, she reminded herself. She had to be confident. She tried again. 'I'm Leah, one of Dot's friends from . . . the circus. I think I might have an idea that will let you play your football match.'

Edie raised an eyebrow, unconvinced, but she gestured for Leah to continue.

Leah took a deep breath. 'You're all trying to come up with different ways to get into the stadium to play your match, but why don't you just play it somewhere else?'

There was silence in the changing room. The players all looked at her blankly, and Leah tried not to imagine William Riley in all of their faces. She forced herself to continue.

'The officials have banned you from playing in an official stadium, but they don't own all the parks and fields in Crickle End, do they? Couldn't you just relocate the match? You'd be able to play whilst still following their rules.'

A low, excited murmur ran through the room. A few of the players exchanged looks, smiles blossoming on their faces.

'Hey!' Mimi exclaimed. 'You already have the perfect location – here!'

'You can't be serious.' Mary looked appalled at the suggestion.

'No, Mimi's right. You have a field that already has pitch markings on it, and a changing room, too.' Dot agreed enthusiastically, almost hopping from foot to foot.

Some of the players were murmuring their agreement.

'Don't be ridiculous. This is a *training* ground,' Mary interjected, speaking slowly as if they might not understand her. She gestured at the players around her. 'We're a professional team. We can't just play on any old field. It's not even properly level.'

'Of course, we can,' Edie was smiling broadly. 'The children are right. As long as we can play, I don't care where we are. This isn't about some big fancy stadium, it's about doing what we love, even when everyone else is trying to stop us.'

Mary narrowed her eyes, sneering at Edie's back. 'I can't believe you're even considering this, but I suppose you're the boss, *captain*.' Leah wasn't sure she meant the words kindly.

Things moved quickly then. Edie took charge of the practical details, and it was decided that the match would be played the day after tomorrow. They'd need to drum up a crowd, and everyone was happy to spread the news discreetly, making sure it didn't reach the ears of a certain Mr Smelting and his associates.

Leah couldn't help the smile that split her face as she watched the team plan, knowing that she'd helped them. Their excitement was contagious and she found herself wishing that they could stay to see the match when it happened. They'd be long gone by then, though – the watch would sweep them back into the future once the clock hit midnight. Or at least, that was the plan.

'Wait,' said Sarah, just as Edie had declared that they were almost done for the evening. 'We're forgetting something. The kits! We still don't have the lucky kits! We can't play against Whitebridge without them. They're so good, we're going to need all the luck we can get!'

There was a collective groan and Dot buried her chin into her chest as several pairs of eyes swivelled to stare at her accusingly.

'We'll just have to wear the training tops,' Edie answered reluctantly.

'We can't!' Sarah protested. 'It has to be the first kits! We'll lose otherwise.'

'Oh, don't be so superstitious, Sarah,' Jo, one of the players, replied. 'We're good enough to do it without them.'

Eventually, the team started to pack up their things. The church bells in town began to toll. *Dong, dong, dong, dong, dong.* Five o'clock. It had only been an hour since they'd left Mr Smelting's office, but it felt like forever had passed inside the little hut. Leah stifled a yawn. It had been a long day and she hadn't realised how tired she actually was.

'Dot!' Edie's voice called over to them. 'Could you and your friends come over here, please?'

The four of them, plus Rolo, trotted over to where Edie was waiting by her table. She gave them all a soft smile as they approached. 'Firstly, I just want to apologise. We weren't very welcoming when you all turned up. I'm sorry about that.'

'It's okay,' Leah smiled. 'We understand that you're under a lot of pressure.'

'Still, that's not the way any of us were raised. We all forgot our manners this evening.' Edie brushed a stray curl behind her ear as her expression suddenly became grave. 'However, Dot, you've got some explaining to do.'

Dot grimaced. 'I'm sorry, Edie. It really was an accident.'

Edie held up a placating hand. 'I know that, and so do the rest of the team. But you might want to lie low for a while. Just until you've made it up to them.'

'I'll do anything,' Dot nodded eagerly.

'In fact,' Edie said, rubbing her chin in thought. 'I might just have a job for you all that could help with that.'

'We can do it! We'll do anything to help!' Dot agreed excitedly. Belatedly, she cast a look behind her at Leah, Mimi and George. Her expression was pleading. 'Won't we?'

Leah fought to hide her grin. Somehow, she suspected that Edie had known Dot would react like this. 'Of course.'

'Well, there's so much to do with organising the new match, but there's one thing I didn't mention. Our opponents, the Whitebridge Ladies, are due to leave Crickle End today. Would you four be able to get to the train station and stop them? I'm sure as soon as you explain our plan, they'll be more than happy to stay for a couple of days more.'

Leah had forgotten entirely that for there to be a match, there needed to be two teams. It would be a disaster if the Whitebridge Ladies boarded that train!

'We're on it!' Mimi said.

Edie beamed. 'Good! But you'd better get going. The train is scheduled to leave in thirty minutes!'

CHAPTER 14:
BACK ON TRACK

The town raced by in a blur as Leah, Mimi and George sprinted through the streets in Dot's wake. Rolo loped along after them, his tongue lolling happily from his mouth. Leah's arms pumped furiously as she willed her legs to go faster, to reach the train station in time.

'How much further?' George panted, his camera bouncing on its straps around his neck. Leah was glad he'd asked. In the future, she could have found her way to the station with her eyes closed, but back in 1921, all of the buildings were different. She found it hard to get her bearings — she was itching to look at Charlie's map again.

'Not long! Just around this corner!' Dot shouted. George gave a huff of relief.

'Woah!' Leah cried as she ran straight into Dot, who had stopped running. The smaller girl was barely sweating after their mad dash.

'We're here! We made it!' Dot said, grinning broadly.

Leah looked around, searching for the familiar glass structure of the train station, but all she could see was a quaint whitewashed building. An iron spire jutted up from the middle of its roof, a clock sitting proudly below the delicate point. 'Where?'

'There!' Dot pointed directly in front of them.

'That's not the station,' George argued.

He was right. This looked nothing like the train station in the Crickle End that they knew. Where were the big glass windows and the corrugated metal roof? Where was the coffee shop that sold those delicious lemon pastries Leah and her mum liked to treat themselves to every time they walked past?

'Of course, it is,' Dot replied, giving them a quizzical look. As if to prove her words, there was the unmistakable piercing whistle of a steam train, followed by a billow of steam rising up into the air. Leah, Mimi and George exchanged bewildered glances. So much had changed in a hundred years!

'Come on,' Dot said, gesturing them forward. She pointed towards the clock. 'We've only got a few minutes before that train leaves and we don't want to miss the team's departure because we've been gawking around outside.'

Just as they were about to enter, Mimi suddenly stopped. 'Wait!' she called, gesturing behind her. At her heels, Rolo sat back on his haunches, his tail wagging as he stared up at them all.

Mimi crouched down, taking his head in her hands and rubbing her fingers over his ears. 'I don't think you can come in here with us, buddy,' she said. Rolo whined forlornly. 'But if you wait here for us, we'll be back soon!' His ears pricked up and he panted happily. His tail resumed its wagging.

The interior of the station was just as alien as the outside. Gone was the yellowing linoleum floor, replaced by shiny mottled marble. The walls were all covered in glossy green tiles that seemed to change colour when the fading light hit them. Instead of a ticket machine, there were three ticketing booths in the western wall, their glass fronts showing three ticket men positioned inside. A small queue of people waited in line to be called forward. George whipped his camera up to his eye, snapping a picture of the scene.

'There's the train!' he exclaimed suddenly. Through an arch they could see the boxy compartments of the train, the doors open ready to welcome its passengers.

'Quick,' Dot said. 'Follow me, before we miss it!'

The four of them charged towards the arch but before they could take a step out onto the platform, a shout brought them up short.

'Hey! What do you think you're doing?'

A burly train guard stood to the side, checking tickets. He marched towards them. A white handlebar moustache dangled over his mouth, the wispy ends dancing at the corners of his lips.

Leah and Dot looked at each other in panic.

Leah licked her lips. 'Um, sorry, sir. We just need to get onto the platform for a moment. There's a really important message we need to deliver.'

'Tickets?' The guard looked at them expectantly.

'No, we don't actually want to get *on* the train. We just need to speak to someone on the platform,' Mimi said urgently. 'We're running out of time!'

The guard snorted, his moustache flapping with his breath. 'You lot must think I was born yesterday. No one gets onto the platform without a ticket.' He straightened his cap imperiously.

The children exchanged an exasperated look. 'We promise we're not lying to you!' Dot told him. 'You could even walk out with us if you don't believe us.'

'I don't have time to do that! I'm already racking up a queue.' He gestured to the spot where he'd been standing, where a line of people was beginning to form, yellow tickets clutched in impatient hands.

'But–'

The guard shook his head firmly. 'No ticket, no platform.' He turned away, the heels of his well-polished shoes clicking on the marble as he strode back to his post.

'What are we going to do now?' George cried. They reluctantly turned back the way they came, pausing in the station doorway and staring dejectedly at each other. Rolo trotted towards them, stopping at Mimi's side and giving her hand a lick.

'We've got to get onto that platform,' Dot said desperately. 'If we don't, the team will kick me out for sure! I'm lucky that Edie even trusted me with this in the first place.'

'HELP!' Mimi suddenly bellowed, throwing her hands in the air. Her face was contorted in an expression of distress. 'HELP!'

Leah, George and Dot stared at her as if she'd lost her mind. 'Mimi!' George whispered frantically. 'What are you doing?'

'Creating a distraction!' Mimi hissed back. She raised her voice again. 'HELP! That man just stole my bag!' She pointed off into the distance.

At her shout, people had begun to turn towards her. A few of them started forward, concern etched on their features. It was working!

'As soon as that ticket guard leaves his post, get onto that platform,' Mimi whispered urgently. 'I don't know how long I'll be able to keep this up, so you'll need to be quick.' The others gave her a determined nod and Mimi resumed her performance, gesticulating wildly as more and more people flocked towards her. At her side, Rolo gave an enthusiastic bark.

Leah, Dot and George edged their way back into the station. Leah kept a close eye on the guard. He was watching the commotion by the door, a frown creasing his forehead. For a moment, Leah worried that he'd ignore the disturbance, but finally, with an irritated *humph*, he strode forward, hands on hips, to see what was causing such a ruckus.

'He's gone!' Leah whispered triumphantly. 'Quick, before he comes back!'

Crouching, the three children scurried across the station lobby. Leah cast one nervous look back over her shoulder before heading through the arch, but everyone's attention was fully focused on Mimi's increasingly dramatic cries. Grinning, Leah skipped through after Dot and George.

The platform was crowded with people and luggage, but that wasn't what caught Leah's attention. It was the magnificent steam train, painted a deep, blood red, that was waiting for them to board. Leah's mouth hung open in awe. She'd never seen anything like it. At the front, the tubular form of the locomotive gleamed. Steam puffed from the chimney, so thick and fluffy she almost felt like she might be able to grab it with her bare hands.

The train gave a sudden whistle, as if telling her that it was happy she had arrived. Leah couldn't help the elated smile that spread over her face . . . until she realised that meant the train would be leaving soon.

'Woah,' George breathed, his camera already in position.

'I can't see the team,' Dot said anxiously. 'Can you?'

Leah scanned the crowded platform, but it was no use. There were too many people. How were they supposed to find the team in the hubbub? Her eyes flicked towards the impressive form of the train and an idea began to develop.

'We need to get on the train,' she announced. 'They must have already boarded.'

'No way!' George replied. 'It's due to leave at any minute! We'll get stuck!'

'Not if we're quick!' Leah said, and before either Dot or George could stop her, she darted to the nearest carriage door and yanked it open.

The steam train was nothing like the grey, plastic trains Leah had been on before. The left of the carriage was split into small compartments containing two benches facing each other with luggage racks overhead. A small table protruded from the wall and a delicate fringed lamp balanced atop. Some carriages were already occupied, passengers having stowed their luggage and settled themselves down for their journey. Outside of the compartments, though, the passageway was still busy with people trying to find their seats.

'Excuse me! Sorry!' Leah called as she wedged her way through, ducking and diving around bodies. From the startled cries and indignant protests she could hear behind her, Leah guessed that Dot and George had followed her into the carriage.

Gradually, they worked their way down the length of the train, hopping from carriage to carriage. With every passing compartment that didn't contain the Whitebridge Ladies, Leah felt herself growing more desperate. They were running out of time!

Suddenly Leah heard a shout from Dot. 'There! I can see them! In the black and white football shirts!'

Leah squinted, looking down the length of the compartment. She caught a flash of stripes – Dot was right! There they were, in the very last carriage. Leah put on a burst of speed, shimmying her way past ladies in voluminous skirts and squeezing behind a very cross-looking gentleman, before bursting into the final compartment.

It seemed the Whitebridge Ladies had booked the entire carriage. Some were already settled in their seats, whilst others helped with stowing the luggage. They all paused at the sight of Leah.

'Can we help you?' one of the women asked, as Dot and George stumbled into the carriage behind Leah.

'We're looking for the team captain,' Leah said a little breathlessly.

A tall blonde woman stepped out from the nearest compartment, one eyebrow raised. 'That's me, Molly Saunders. What can I do for you?'

Dot sighed in relief. 'I've got a message from Edie Partridge. She sent us to ask you if you'll stay in Crickle End for another few days. We're going to rearrange the final match!'

Molly frowned in confusion, 'But the officials . . .'

'We've got a plan,' Leah told her excitedly. 'One that means the officials won't be able to stop you from playing!'

Molly stared at them. Behind her, the team were shifting restlessly, exchanging perplexed looks. 'Is this some kind of joke?' Molly said finally. 'We've already come a long way for this game, and we're tired of being mucked around.'

'It's not a trick!' Leah protested loudly. 'Edie really has sent us.'

'Uh, Leah . . .' George's voice sounded anxious. The train had started to groan, and outside on the platform Leah heard the pipe of the conductor's whistle as the train prepared to depart.

'Look,' Leah said urgently. She knew this was her only chance to convince Molly and the team. 'We don't have a lot of time. Either you can believe us, and you still have a chance to take the trophy home, or you can throw this opportunity away and leave Crickle End empty-handed. It's up to you.' Her heart was racing. She'd never spoken to an adult like that before.

Molly was silent for a moment. Then she sighed and shook her head. 'Come on, kids,' she said, moving forward and ushering them out of the carriage door. The train gave a despondent puff of smoke as they stepped back down onto the platform. Leah's shoulders slumped. They'd failed. Edie was going to be so disappointed in them.

Then Leah realised that Molly hadn't disappeared back into the carriage. Instead, she was hanging out of the doorway, waving her hand urgently at the conductor. 'Stop the train!' she shouted. Then she grinned down at Leah, George and Dot. 'There's been a change of plan.'

CHAPTER 15: A NIGHT-TIME ADVENTURE

When Leah, Dot and George emerged back onto the street, most of the crowd had filtered away. A few still lingered, though, most notably the station guard, his moustache quivering as he stared down at Mimi, with his hands on his hips.

Mimi was still engrossed in her performance. 'I think it's too late, sir,' she proclaimed, tossing her head back in mock dismay. 'They've already gone. I don't think I'll ever get my bag back now.'

Leah and George stifled their giggles as they stopped at her side.

'Where have you three been?' the guard asked suspiciously.

'We've been looking for the thief,' George replied, his voice and expression flat.

'But we didn't find them,' Leah said to Mimi, trying to sound apologetic.

Mimi sighed, holding a hand to her forehead. 'Thank you for trying.' She held out her hand to the train guard. 'And thank you, sir, for coming to my aid. I don't know what I would have done without you.'

Bemused, the guard took her hand and shook it. Giving him a wave, the four of them turned their back on him, stifling their giggles as they crossed the road. Rolo followed them. Leah looked back over her shoulder before they disappeared around the corner to see the guard still standing there watching them, scratching his head in suspicious confusion.

'Did you reach the team in time?' Mimi asked, pausing to pat the golden stray on the head.

'We sure did,' George grinned.

Mimi sighed in relief. 'Phew! Edie's going to be so pleased!'

'Maybe this means my chances of joining the team one day aren't completely ruined,' Dot said. 'I might still be in with a chance.'

Leah started to agree, but her mouth was distorted by an enormous yawn. The events of the day suddenly crashed down on her and she felt *exhausted*.

Dot yawned too, stretching her arms above her head. 'It's been a very long day. We should head home.'

Leah felt a twinge in her chest at the word 'home'. It wouldn't be long before they'd be able to go home too! There were only a few more hours until midnight and then the watch would whisk them back to their own time.

George seemed to be thinking the same thing. 'We need to get home too, L.' He frowned. 'My mum's going to be so worried.'

'Plus we've got the big match coming up! We can't miss that!' Mimi added.

Leah turned to Dot. 'Remember that watch we told you about, Dot? The one that brought us here from the future?'

Dot rolled her eyes. 'You're not still going on about this future thing, are you?'

'You might not believe us, but at midnight it's

going to take us all back home. Do you know anywhere we can stay while we wait?'

Dot shrugged. 'You can come home with me until you work things out.'

'Would that be okay? We don't want to intrude.'

'You won't be. I've got so many brothers, I'm sure Mum won't mind a few extras.'

As Dot led the way back to her house, the streets of Crickle End were quiet, its residents trickling back to their houses. When they arrived in front of the familiar terrace row, the window of Dot's front room emanated a soft rosy glow. Dot let Rolo into the garden through the side gate, then she unlocked the front door, ushering them all inside.

Inside, the living room was toasty warm, the modest fire that was roaring in the grate providing both light and heat. Four lanky forms occupied most of the space – two in armchairs, and the other two stretching out across the rug. If possible, it seemed even smaller than it had earlier, with so many extra bodies crammed into the space. In the kitchen Leah could hear someone busily banging about.

'Dotty!' One of the boys on the rug exclaimed, jumping to his feet. He had hair the same colour as Dot, and freckles to match, although he was a few years older than they were. 'Where have you been?'

'This is Johnny,' Dot said. 'And that's Harry, and Edward. You've met Charlie already.' Charlie gave a lazy wave as she pointed out her brothers. 'These are my new friends, Leah, Mimi and George.'

'Nice to meet you,' said Johnny, grinning broadly. On the carpet, Harry lifted his head from his book with a slight smile. Edward, who seemed to be engrossed in a crossword puzzle in the newspaper, didn't look at them at all.

'Dot!' came an admonishing voice. 'You're late! Look at that sky! Do you see a sun amongst those clouds?' A woman had appeared in the doorway to the kitchen. She looked exactly like Dot, the only difference being that where Dot's hair was straight, her mother's was curly.

'Sorry, Ma,' Dot grimaced. 'It was an accident.' She shuffled over towards her mother and gave her an apologetic hug. Her mother sighed and shook her head in mock despair, even as she patted her daughter lovingly on the head.

'An accident you'd best not have any business repeating, missy! You know the rules.' She paused, suddenly realising that there were more children in her living room than usual. 'Oh, you've brought home some friends!'

'This is Leah, Mimi and George. Do you think they'd be able to stay with us for a few days? They've come into town with the circus, but . . . their tent got ripped. They don't have anywhere to go.' The white lie tripped easily off Dot's tongue. Leah prayed that her mother wouldn't ask for a demonstration of their circus skills.

'Of course, they can!' Dot's mum said. 'You can call me Mrs Andrews.'

Mrs Andrews led them through into the kitchen, where they all scrubbed their hands with lukewarm water and a rough, scratchy soap. The boys all filed in after, and there was a slight commotion as more chairs were crammed in around the circular dining table. Finally, they were all seated, and Dot's mother took a big dish from the oven. There was a golden pie inside, its pastry burnished bronze. Next came a vat of potatoes mashed and whipped into fluffy cream peaks. Leah felt her mouth watering as she realised she hadn't eaten anything since the toast she'd hurriedly grabbed that morning.

Dot's brothers dug in with little ceremony. Johnny heaped mounds of potato onto his plate, whilst Edward hacked at his mother's immaculate pie crust with a sharp knife, spooning out the chunks of carrot and meat within.

'Oh no,' Mimi murmured under her breath.

'What's the matter?' Leah asked. Johnny shook the potato spoon at her and she held out her plate to receive a generous dumping of starchy mash.

'That's a meat pie, isn't it?' Mimi grimaced and Leah winced sympathetically. Mimi was a vegetarian.

'Just do your best,' Leah whispered back. 'Maybe you can eat some of the crust on the side that hasn't touched the meat. I'm not sure people from the 1920s will understand what a vegetarian is.'

Mimi puckered her lips.

'So, you guys are from the circus?' Harry asked.

Leah bit her lip. 'Uh, yeah. We just joined recently.'

'What do you do?' Charlie asked before shoving a fork full of pie into his mouth.

Mimi beamed and opened her mouth, but George jumped in before she could reply. 'We just run errands for the performers. Nothing important.'

'But one day we'll be on the big stage,' Mimi interjected, shooting George a petulant glare. 'I'm going to be a contortionist.' Leah couldn't stop the laugh that escaped her mouth, but she managed to turn it into an unconvincing cough. Mimi was the least-flexible person she knew. She couldn't even touch her toes successfully.

'Something really exciting happened today, Mum,' Dot jumped in, before Mimi's little embellishments could get them into trouble.

'The team decided to play the final match of the season!'

Charlie frowned. 'But I thought women's football's been banned?'

'It has,' George answered. 'But only in official stadiums and tournaments. The team aren't going to play in an official stadium.'

'They're going to use the training ground, instead.' Dot was talking animatedly now, waving her cutlery above her head. Gravy droplets flew everywhere, one splattering Johnny's cheek, much to his disgust. 'So the Champions will have the chance to win the cup again this year!'

'That's such good news,' Mrs Andrews said happily.

'Is it?' Edward interrupted. He wrinkled his nose. 'If you ask me, I think it's a good thing they've introduced the ban.'

'Well, no one was asking you,' Charlie retorted.

Harry shrugged. 'Maybe Edward's right. It's not very respectable, is it? All those women running around like that.'

'I don't see what's wrong with it,' Leah

challenged him. 'We've got just as much right to play as you do.'

'It's not about rights,' Edward argued. 'It's about what's appropriate.'

'Well, I don't think you're being very appropriate,' Dot snapped. 'I think you're being stupid.'

Edward opened his mouth angrily but Mrs Andrews interrupted. 'Alright, that's enough you lot. No arguing at the dinner table.' She paused and then continued, 'It doesn't sit right with me, though, all those people in suits deciding what women are and aren't allowed to do. And the Champions are such a good team.' She turned to Leah, George and Mimi. 'We're all very proud of them, no matter what the boys say.'

'Will you tell your friends, Ma?' Dot asked, ignoring Edward's angry frown. 'We want to make sure as many people as possible are there to watch the game on Thursday.'

'Of course,' Mrs Andrews smiled. 'I'm sure they'll all be very eager to see the Champions play for the town.'

The conversation turned to other things after that, and when they'd all finished eating, Mrs Andrews sent them upstairs to get ready for bed. Leah yawned widely when Dot let them into her room.

'I'm so tired,' she said, rubbing her eyes. 'I can't wait to shut my eyes and go to sleep.'

'Sleep?' Dot shot her an incredulous look. 'I don't think so. We've got other plans tonight!'

Mimi gaped at her. 'What else could we possibly need to do?'

'We need to try the watch again,' George pointed out, his hand going to his pocket. 'As soon as the clock strikes midnight, we should be able to go home.'

Dot shook her head in irritation. 'No, that's not what I meant. I'm talking about the circus!'

'The circus?' Leah raised her eyebrow.

'I do this every year,' Dot told her patiently. 'When the circus rolls into town, I always sneak out on the first night. Mum and Dad would never let me go otherwise.'

Leah considered for a moment. She was very

tired, her limbs heavy, but how often would she get to visit a circus, let alone a circus in the 1920s? She grinned at Dot. 'Go on then,' she said. 'But we've got to make sure we don't miss midnight!' They needed to get home.

They followed Dot out of her bedroom and onto the landing, treading lightly so that her mum and brothers wouldn't hear them. Dot paused outside the door next to her own and gently eased it open. One by one, they slipped through into the darkness.

'This is my parents' room,' she explained, guiding them through the gloom. 'As I don't have a window in my room, I usually sneak out of this one.'

'We're going out of a window?' George squeaked, his voice high with panic.

'Don't worry,' Dot reassured him. 'There's a shed underneath. It's not a long drop.'

Dot eased the window open and beckoned them all over to look outside. A couple of metres below Leah could make out the flat roof of Dot's garden shed, and just beyond that she could see

Rolo's shadowy form, jumping about excitedly as he spotted them.

'All you need to do is drop down and land on there, and then you can hop into the garden. I'll go first, so you can see.'

Dot hitched up her dress, holding it in one hand as she levered herself easily up onto the windowsill. Without any hesitation she pushed herself out and landed with a thump on the shed roof. Carefully, she scooted along so that she was sat with her legs dangling over the edge of the shed and pushed off, landing with a little stumble in the garden below. She made it look easy.

'I don't think I can do that,' George whispered to Leah, his voice quivering. 'I don't like heights.'

Leah gave him a reassuring smile. 'It's okay, George. We'll go first so you can just copy what we do.'

Mimi went next, and then Leah. Both of them landed neatly on the grass.

George peered out of the window and shook his head. Leah called up, 'If you get to the shed, I promise I'll help you down to the garden. I know you can do it!'

Finally, he nodded, and after a few more minutes all four of them were in the garden. Rolo ran around their feet, letting out excited yips.

'Here,' Dot said, gesturing them towards the back fence. There was a row of bushes growing against it, and behind them was a stack of bikes. They were similar to Leah's bike at home, but the tyres were thinner and some of the handlebars were going rusty. Dot grabbed a discoloured white one and gestured to the rest. 'They're my brothers' but they won't mind if you borrow them tonight.'

Once they'd all selected a bike, Dot opened the gate and led them out into a little alley. She began to cycle towards the street and the others followed her, Rolo easily keeping pace. They turned left, heading away from the centre of town, and went through dark streets lit by streetlamps.

'Those have just been fitted,' Dot said, gesturing to the giraffe-necked lights. 'It makes it so much easier to see where you're going now!'

Even without the streetlamps, though, it would

have been impossible to miss the circus. As they left the town behind them and the tarmac roads gave way to rugged dirt tracks, the lights around the tent lit the night sky. They could hear the music dancing in the air, could see the spotlights tracking across the sky. Dot gave a whoop and began to pedal faster. Leah followed her, feeling excitement grow in her belly. She was going to the circus!

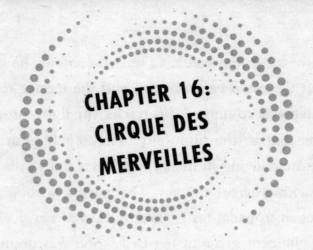

CHAPTER 16:
CIRQUE DES MERVEILLES

The circus moved with a life of its own.

After they'd stashed their bikes in a nearby bush, the four of them made a beeline for the entrance. Stepping beneath its draped arch felt like taking a plunge into an entirely different world. It was a head-spinning mixture of sights and sounds, a busy kaleidoscope of beautiful jewel tones, swirling together.

They wandered aimlessly, gaping at the wonders around them. In one direction a clown juggled too many balls for Leah to count. The crowd gathered around him sang a chorus of *oohs* and *aahs* as he added another ball to those spinning dizzily around his head. Then Leah laughed and nudged Mimi as she caught sight of a contortionist performing by another tent, her legs curled up over her head like a snail shell. George snapped a picture of a fire-breather, the flames streaming from his mouth in a plume that was so hot, Leah could almost feel the heat against her cheek. Interspersed between the performers were a variety of stalls, hawking wares such as sweet

roasted nuts, or pink clouds of sticky candy floss. The whole place felt like a maze, with various paths taking them off in different directions, turning them around so that Leah had no idea which way they'd come.

'Look,' said Dot, pointing. Leah followed the direction of her finger. At the end of the path in front of them, a great structure rose above the other tents. Red-and-white-striped fabric reached up towards the sky, the canvas sides sweeping down to the floor like a giant skirt. 'It's the Big Top!'

'I've never been to the circus before, Dot,' Leah admitted. 'What's the Big Top?'

Dot's eyes lit up with excitement. 'The Big Top is the centre of it all! That's where you can see all the best acts. The Lion Tamer, the Human Cannonball – all the really exciting stuff!'

Leah stared up at the giant tent in amazement. 'That sounds incredible! Can we go there next?'

Dot's face fell. 'We can't actually go in, Leah. You've got to pay an entry fee.'

'Oh,' Mimi's mouth was pursed in

disappointment. 'We don't have any money.' She gave a wistful sigh. 'I would have loved to have seen real performers at work.'

'I can't believe we've got this one chance to visit a circus in the 1920s and we don't even get to see the good bit,' George whined, echoing Leah's frustration.

'Hang on!' Leah tilted her head as she stared at her friends, an idea blossoming in her mind.

'Uh oh,' Mimi said. 'I know that look.'

'I've had an idea!' Leah exclaimed, pulling them all in closer. 'We don't have any money right now. But we could earn some, couldn't we?'

George frowned. 'How?'

Leah gestured around, her arm taking in all the tents and circus people. 'There are performers *everywhere*. So why don't we become performers too?'

'Brilliant,' Mimi breathed.

'But we don't have anything to perform,' Dot pointed out.

'Not yet, we don't,' Leah agreed. 'But we're all pretty smart. We should be able to come up with something, right?'

There was silence as the four of them weighed up their options.

'I know!' Mimi cried suddenly. 'What if we did some fancy football tricks?'

'People aren't going to pay to see that! Loads of people can do football tricks!' Leah said, shaking her head. 'Mimi, why don't you perform a section from one of your plays or something?'

Mimi suddenly blushed and shook her head furiously, her braids whipping about her face. 'No, I can't do that. I'd need a full cast with me to do it right.'

Dot suddenly gasped. 'I've got it!' she exclaimed, smiling. She pointed at George. 'We can take pictures with George's fancy camera!'

George looked dubiously at the camera hanging around his neck. 'This? Do you really think people would pay for that?'

'Of course,' Dot nodded firmly. 'We don't have cameras like that around here. Everyone will be desperate to get their hands on one of your photos.'

'Do you have enough film for that, George?' Mimi asked.

George nodded, patting his backpack. 'I always carry a stash of extra paper for the camera with me.'

Leah shrugged. 'Let's give it a go. What's the worst that can happen?'

It took them a while to find a space that wasn't already taken up by another performer or a stall, but they eventually tucked themselves away next to a tent belonging to a fortune teller.

'Right,' Mimi said, clapping her hands together. 'Let's go and find us some customers!' She strode out into the crowds without waiting for Leah to follow her.

'Excuse me, ma'am,' Mimi stopped a lady with a peacock-blue hat perched atop her steely grey hair. 'You look like just the type of lady who'd be interested in having her irresistible glamour immortalised in a once-in-a-lifetime souvenir!'

Mimi and Leah spread out along the road, pointing potential customers towards the ever-growing queue near where they had left George.

They could hear gasps of amazement as their friend demonstrated exactly what the strange contraption around his neck could do. It turned out that Rolo was quite the selling point too – despite his scruffy appearance, almost everyone wanted him to star in their picture. He obliged, his tail wagging and his tongue hanging happily between his teeth. Dot guided each customer out. As they beamed in wonder at the small rectangular photograph in their hands, she told them all about a very special football match scheduled for a couple of days' time.

It wasn't long before Dot declared they had more than enough money to get all of them into the Big Top.

'Entrance is a penny each. Which means . . .' she counted out the mixture of coins in her hand. 'That we have enough to get some candy floss, too!'

'My favourite!' Mimi grinned.

With pink whirls of spun sugar clutched tightly in their hands, the four of them joined the stream of revellers heading towards the Big

Top. At the door, a performer whose face was painted with black and white diamonds took their coins, handing them a blue ticket in exchange. Surprisingly, Rolo was allowed in too.

Once inside, Leah stared up in wonder as the fabric of the tent reached towards the gloomy sky, coming together at an impossibly tall point. The centre of the Big Top was dominated by a huge empty ring, and its floor was covered with sand.

Dot managed to find them a vacant bench right at the front, and just a few moments after they'd sat down, the torches that edged the sand ring sprang into life. The audience gasped in wonder. There was a flash of light and a bloom of smoke and then a figure seemed to magically appear in the centre. Clothed in a vibrant red suit and wearing one of the most impressive top hats she'd ever seen, Leah guessed he must be the ringmaster. His black moustache was oiled into two perfect curls and his ruddy cheeks bunched up as he smiled. His dark eyes sparkled with mischief.

'I've got to get this on camera,' George said. His sticky fingers fumbled to raise his camera to his eyes.

'Good evening, ladies and gentlemen!' the ringmaster proclaimed. His voice boomed all around the tent and Leah felt a flicker of envy at how confident and effortless he seemed. 'Welcome to Cirque des Merveilles! Tonight you will witness sights you'd only expect to see in your dreams. You'll feel things that will tingle your senses and tantalise your imagination. My performers will dazzle and delight, taking you to places you will never again visit in your lifetime. So, sit back, relax, and leave your lives behind for a few short hours. Let the show begin!'

The crowd roared as the torches flared, their flames soaring even higher. Sparklers erupted alongside them and the audience let out an appreciative *oooh* as four clowns appeared on unicycles. They rode around the edge of the ring, their hands busily throwing juggling balls.

The next hour passed in a whirlwind. Performer after performer emerged into the ring, each better than the last. Leah gasped as the tightrope walker wobbled her way along a wire so thin it was barely visible. She gaped as the strongman lifted a weighted bar that had three contortionists and a clown balancing on top of it. She leaned forward in amazement, her fingers gripping the edge of the bench, as a short man wearing a leotard led a lion three times his size through different obstacles and exercises. Leah had seen lions in the zoo, but she'd always been behind a glass panel; being so close now was both terrifying and exhilarating.

By the time the show came to an end, Leah's cheeks hurt so much from smiling. She, Dot, Mimi and George followed the crowd out of the tent. Their faces and fingers were sticky with the remnants of their candy floss, but none of them cared.

'That was so cool!' George exclaimed.

'I can't believe how good those performers were!' Mimi said dreamily. 'I wish I could do *half* the things they did!'

Dot beamed. 'That was the best show I've been

to yet! Even better than last year.'

Suddenly a voice boomed out across the circus grounds. It sounded tinny, as if it was coming through a megaphone. 'Attention, ladies and gentlemen. As it has almost reached midnight, Cirque des Merveilles will soon be closing. Please make your way to the exit as soon as possible. We look forward to seeing you again soon.'

Leah couldn't believe the night had passed so quickly. They'd been having so much fun she'd barely been aware of the minutes flying by.

'Midnight?' George gasped. 'It's almost time to try the pocket watch again!'

'You're right,' Leah exclaimed. 'We should hurry. It's time to go home!'

'Why don't we head back to the bikes?' Mimi suggested. 'It'll be nice and quiet there.'

The others agreed and they rushed back underneath the circus's draped entrance, Rolo trotting along at their heels. Outside, everything seemed plain and drab compared to the wonders of Cirque des Merveilles.

Dot led them back to the cluster of bushes

where they'd hidden the bikes. When they arrived, she turned to face them all. 'Don't you think you're all taking this a bit far now?' she asked.

'What do you mean?' George replied, confused.

'I know you're not really from the future. You don't need to keep up the act.'

'No, Dot, we really . . .' Leah trailed off and gave a sigh. She wasn't going to convince Dot with words, she realised. Her friend needed to see it to believe it. 'Never mind. George, do you have the watch?'

George fished in his shirt pocket, pulling out the silver chain and the pocket watch attached to the end. Behind them, the lights of the circus began to dim, plunging the field into a deeper gloom. In the distance, the bells of the town started to ring. Almost twelve o'clock.

Leah wound the crown of the watch, the hands moving into position. When it was ready, she turned to face Dot.

'Thank you so much for everything you've done for us,' she said. 'We wouldn't have got very far without you.'

'We'll really miss you,' George added.

Mimi nodded her agreement and then burst out, 'Please look after Rolo! I don't want him to go back onto the streets.' She crouched down to stare into the dog's eyes, her fingers buried in the fur around his ears. Rolo gave her a big lick across the face and Mimi giggled.

Dot shook her head, but she looked more uncertain now. 'I know this is all some big joke . . .' she said. Her voice trailed off.

Leah didn't reply. Instead, she held the watch out to Mimi and George. They each took hold. Leah took a deep breath. Finally, they were going home; they wouldn't miss the big football match and she'd get to see her parents. As the final bell rang, she clicked the crown twice and squeezed her eyes shut, readying herself for the stomach-turning plunge into time.

Nothing happened.

Leah cracked open an eyelid. They were still in the field, with Dot standing in front of them and Rolo sat expectantly at her feet. It hadn't worked.

Leah clicked the crown again, and again, and again, but no matter how many times she pressed the little button, they were still firmly in 1921.

'I told you!' Dot cried triumphantly, punching the air. 'You can't fool me!'

George burst into tears.

He buried his face in his hands. 'Why isn't it working?' he wailed. 'We're never going to get home!'

Mimi put her arms around him, pulling him in close. 'Don't say that, George,' she said. Leah could tell she was trying to sound brave, even though her bottom lip was wobbling, too. 'We'll figure it out. We won't be stuck here forever.' She looked desperately at Leah. 'Will we?'

Leah didn't know what to say. She stared at the watch in her hand, willing it to give her some kind of clue. Instead, all she could see were the fading circus lights reflected in its glass face.

'Maybe . . . maybe it's not working because it's not time for you to go home, yet,' said Dot. The triumph had drained from her face, and now she was looking at George with a concerned expression. It was as if seeing his reaction had been the one thing to convince her that the whole thing might not be a hoax.

'What?' George croaked, raising his tear-stained face from his hands and staring at her.

Dot shrugged self-consciously. 'All I'm saying is that it brought you here for a reason, didn't it? Maybe you can't get home because you haven't finished what you were meant to do.'

Leah tilted her head. Despite her frustration, she had to admit that did make sense. After all, the watch could have sent them anywhere in time but it had chosen to bring them here. Finally, she nodded. 'Dot's right,' she said slowly. 'Remember the note? "For those who need it most." That's what it said. The watch must think we need to be here for something. And that something just hasn't happened yet.'

'But what if it never happens?' George said, sniffing.

'It will,' said Mimi. 'Why don't we try again tomorrow, just in case?'

'Agreed,' said Leah. 'It's bound to send us home

sooner or later. For now, though, we should head back to Dot's house. It's getting late, and cold.' She hugged her arms around her body, shivering as a breeze blew over the field.

George wiped his cheeks and nodded. They dragged their bikes from behind the bushes and pushed them across the grass towards the road. As they mounted them and began the ride to Dot's home, Leah thought wistfully about her own house, and the comfortable bed waiting for her in her bedroom. She thought of her mum and dad. She wondered if they were out searching for her, worried about where she'd gone. Longing clutched at her stomach and she realised she missed them ferociously.

I wonder if I'll ever see them again?

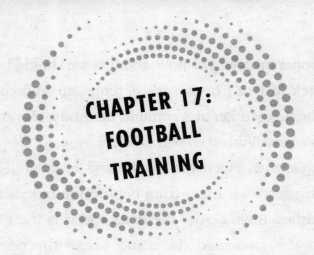

CHAPTER 17: FOOTBALL TRAINING

'Pass me that paint pot, George,' Leah said, pointing towards the white tub at George's feet. He handed it across to her, being careful not to slosh any of the paint over the sides. Leah dipped her paintbrush into the white liquid, then slowly traced over the old, faded penalty spot on the grass.

That morning, they'd all set out for the training field where the Crickle End Champions had gathered to begin their preparations for the match the next day. It was still cold enough that they'd all borrowed coats from Dot, but the grey clouds of the day before had given way to a cautious sun, casting the field in a lemony light. The four of them had quickly been put to work.

Dot and Leah had been instructed to refresh the pitch markings, whilst George drew numbers on the back of the practice shirts and Mimi eagerly volunteered to mow the grass. She marched past them now, pushing the manual mower in front of her. Behind, neat rows of shorn pitch were beginning to appear. Rolo, as ever, trotted along next to her. Mimi had found a red dog collar and it looked very handsome against his white and caramel coat, even if he was still a bit grubby.

George gave a giant yawn. 'I'm so sleepy,' he grumbled.

After the circus, they'd crept back into the house through the front door and crammed themselves into Dot's bedroom. The three girls had slept top-to-toe in the bed, whilst George had curled up on the floor in a great nest of blankets. They'd all woken up heavy eyed.

'It was worth it though, wasn't it?' Mimi grinned. 'I don't think I'll ever see anything as good as that circus!'

'It was amazing,' Leah agreed. 'I keep thinking about that lion. It was so close!'

'It's just a shame about the watch,' George pouted, patting the coat pocket where he'd stored it.

'It's okay,' Leah reassured him. 'It'll work at midday.' Her voice was confident, but her stomach roiled uneasily. What if the watch was broken forever?

Dot watched them all, but she didn't say anything. After a moment, she went back to carefully painting her section of the pitch.

The door to the training room opened and the team spilled out onto the grass. They'd changed out of their casual clothes into their training kits. They all looked much happier than the day before – the prospect of the impending match had lifted their spirits. Leah felt a pang as she watched them. They reminded her of her own football team back home.

'Everyone in my street has agreed to come,' Sarah was saying as they walked towards the children.

'And my brother said he's told everyone at the factory,' Lizzie added. She frowned. 'Not

everyone is thrilled about it, of course, but . . .
word is spreading fast!'

'Hopefully, if we get enough fans, the donations
we receive for entry might be enough to buy us
some new kits and equipment,' Edie told them.

'That would be brilliant,' Sarah sighed. She
plucked at her white shirt; it had seen better days.
The edges were going a strange grey colour. 'We
could do with some new stuff.'

'I hope the first kits turn up eventually, though,'
Jo sighed. 'It doesn't feel right playing a match
without them.'

'I know what you mean,' Sarah said glumly.
'It's just not the same. I can't believe we're going
to have to play in these.'

At the mention of the kits, George stood up,
dusting off his shorts. 'I'm going to help the team
get the training shirts ready for the match,' he
said. 'I have some markers in my bag, so we can
write their names and numbers on the back.' He
marched over towards Mimi and together they
made for the benches by the changing room.

'Shall we help the team set up for their training

session?' Dot asked. She wiped her paintbrush against the side of the pot, scraping off the excess paint.

'Good idea,' Leah said. She grabbed the tub and followed Dot to the rickety equipment shed next to the changing room. It wasn't the sturdiest of structures. The wooden planks were discoloured and some had come loose. Depending on how much profit they made from the match donations, the shed would definitely be on their list of things to fix up.

Some of the women were already inside, grabbing footballs and cones. Leah placed the paint bucket to one side and grabbed a stack of cones.

'Hi, Anna,' she heard Dot say. Leah turned to see that Mary's sister was hovering in the doorway. Now that Leah had spent more time with the team's star striker, she could see that the resemblance between the two was obvious.

'Morning, Dot,' Anna replied. 'Hi, Leah!' She gave an awkward wave and Leah smiled at her. 'Where are Mimi and George?'

'They're helping the team outside,' Dot replied. 'Leah, will you grab that stack of cones for me?' She pointed towards the back of the shed. Leah had to climb over some boxes before she could reach the cones Dot had asked for, but as she did, a glint of gold caught her eye. She paused, squinting.

There was a trophy at the back of the shed. A very *big* trophy.

'What's that?' Leah exclaimed, staring at it in awe.

Dot peered over her shoulder. 'That's the Women's Championship Cup,' she said. Then she added wistfully, 'I've always dreamed of winning that. Lifting it up above my shoulders and taking it home.'

'You've got a long way to go before that'll happen, Dot,' came a haughty voice from behind them. It was Mary. She was standing next to her sister in the shed doorway. Anna seemed to become smaller in her shadow. 'I didn't join the team until I was seventeen.'

'Not that long!' Dot protested. 'I'll be thirteen soon.'

'Well, you never know what's just around the corner,' Edie interjected as she squeezed past Mary, coming into the shed to pick up a bag of footballs. 'It might be yours sooner than you think!' Behind her, Mary rolled her eyes.

'It will!' Dot breathed, her voice determined.

'What's it doing in the back of the shed?' Leah asked. 'It seems too precious to be stuck in here.'

'After the match was cancelled this week, we volunteered to keep it somewhere safe,' Edie told her.

'Is this shed really that secure?' Leah wasn't convinced.

Mary gave a short laugh. 'It might not look it, but there's only one key to this building and our mighty leader has it,' she said sarcastically. 'Even I don't have one. You'd need to steal that first before you could get in here. Anyway, we're wasting time. Let's get out onto the pitch and make the most of the sunshine.'

Dot and Leah followed Mary, Anna and Edie outside. The team were already out on the pitch, passing the balls between them.

Leah paused to watch them in amazement. They moved so fluidly, it was like the ball was an extension of their limbs and each player was a single part of one giant organism. They seemed to know what their teammates were going to do before they'd even moved.

'It's amazing how confident they are,' Leah said to Anna, who had stopped next to her and Dot. 'I'd love to be as good as they are.'

'They practise *a lot*,' Anna said. Her voice was so quiet that Leah had to strain to hear over the team's shouts. 'They're all very dedicated.'

'They must really love football. They wouldn't be able to put so much of themselves into it if they didn't.' Leah mused, almost to herself. She thought about her mum and all of the hours she spent at her law firm's offices, especially when she had a big case to work on. Her dad was the same. He always volunteered to take extra shifts at the hospital if they needed him. Both of them always put their whole heart into their jobs.

Leah thought that sounded quite daunting. Sometimes she struggled to motivate herself to even do her homework.

'It doesn't always come easily, though,' Anna said, as if she could read Leah's mind. Her breath puffed into the cold air and she stamped her booted feet against the floor, trying to warm them up. 'Mary, for instance. She didn't always want to be a footballer. When we were very young, she dreamed of being a greengrocer. But things changed. As soon as she kicked that first football, we all knew she'd discovered what she was meant to do.'

Leah found that strangely reassuring. Even someone as dedicated as Mary hadn't always known where her future was heading. Instead, she'd just followed what she enjoyed. Maybe Leah didn't have to worry so much about the future, yet. Maybe she could experiment and change her mind, just like Mary. That was, if they ever managed to get home, of course. If they couldn't fix the watch, Leah wasn't sure what her future might look like.

'What about you?' she asked Anna, pushing thoughts of the watch aside for the moment.

'Were you like Mary, or did you know that you always wanted to be a footballer?'

A strange expression crossed Anna's face, but before she could reply, Leah heard someone calling her name from across the pitch. It was Edie.

'Why don't you come and join us?' she shouted. 'You and Dot both!'

The two girls exchanged a glance. They grinned at each other. Leah looked for Mimi, but she was still marching the lawn mower up and down the side of the pitch while George repainted the lines. Instead, Leah turned to Anna. 'Do you want to come too?' she asked.

Anna shook her head. 'No that's okay. I've got to . . .' she trailed off, flapping her hand towards the changing room.

'Go and play, Anna!' Mary seemed to have appeared from nowhere. She frowned down at her little sister. 'You could use the practice.'

Anna tugged on one of her plaits and bit her lip. 'No, honestly, Mary. It's okay.'

'Don't be ridiculous!' Mary snapped. 'Get out

there and play!'

'It's okay, Mary,' Leah interrupted. 'Anna can practise with us another time.'

Mary scowled.

'Come on, girls!' Edie called from where she was waiting by the goal. Leah and Dot gave Anna an apologetic wave before they jogged across the pitch towards Edie.

The team's captain had a football waiting at her feet, and she passed it swiftly to Dot as they approached. It bounced off Dot's foot and she kicked it towards Leah, who caught it on the inside of her foot and then passed it back to Edie. As they kicked the ball Leah felt herself relax, the

sounds of the other girls practising fading into the background. The broken pocket watch and the dilemma of how they were going to get home left her mind.

'How did the team start, Edie?' asked Leah once they'd got into a good rhythm, their muscles warming up with the movement. 'Have you all been playing together since you were children?'

Edie shook her head. 'Oh no,' she said. 'Girls' football teams didn't really exist around here when I was small. It was just the boys. But when the war hit . . . everything changed. The men all went off to fight and we were left behind. Most of the Crickle End team you know today met when we were workers in the munitions factory outside of town.'

'What are munitions?' Leah's tongue stumbled over the unfamiliar word.

'Weapons,' Dot supplied, kicking the ball to Edie. 'Guns.'

Edie gave Leah a strange look. 'Haven't you ever heard about the munitions factories before?' she asked.

'Uh . . . we didn't have much to do with the war in the circus,' Leah said, flushing.

'Leah's not from around here, Edie, remember?' Dot said.

Edie nodded and laughed. 'Of course. It's easy to forget. It feels like you've been here forever!' she said. 'Well, usually it would be the men working that sort of big machinery, but almost all of them were away at war. So we ladies stepped in. It wasn't easy work. Rations were tough, London was being attacked by bombers, and if that wasn't bad enough, the burden of knowing our family members were overseas fighting for us . . . it was a difficult time. We needed something to take our minds off it all. That's when we started to play football. It wasn't anything serious to start with, but then we came to rely on it. For lots of us, it became one of the reasons we trudged to that factory every day. It doesn't pay much, and we still have to work second jobs, of course, but it's not about the money.'

'Did the town always support you?'

'It became as important to them as it was to us,'

Edie shrugged, swinging her foot back and deftly kicking the ball to Leah. 'They needed something to distract them all, too.'

'I was only five,' Dot said. 'But I remember going to some of the early matches. It was the highlight of our week. And it wasn't just us. All over the country, women's teams started popping up.'

'And ordinary people loved going to see them play. But when the men came back, all that changed.' Edie sighed regretfully. 'There will always be someone who wants to fight against change and defend the status quo.'

'That's why this ban has happened,' Dot said sadly. 'And because the ladies were making too much money. At least, that's what my Pa says.'

'Enough of this talk,' Edie interrupted, clapping her hands. 'We're here to play football, not jabber all morning. Leah, you're a pretty good footballer. Do they let you play in the circus?'

'Um, we have a small team going,' Leah said, trying to make the half-lie sound convincing. 'But only in our free time.'

'Shall we take some penalties?' Dot asked eagerly. 'I can be in goal and you can shoot!'

Leah tried not to grimace, and her stomach sank. The memory of yesterday's training session flooded back, along with everything she'd felt as she'd stood rooted to the penalty spot.

'That's a great idea, Dot,' Edie replied before Leah could answer. 'Let's see what your shooting skills are like, Leah!'

Dot wasted no time rushing into the goal. Despite being so small, she did an impressive job of filling the space, bouncing on her toes and jumping from side to side. Reluctantly, Leah got into position. Edie threw her the football and she placed it precisely at her feet.

For a moment, Leah didn't move, her eyes glued to the football. Her heart hammered in her chest. When she missed – because she totally knew she would – Dot and Edie would think she was a fraud who was only pretending to be a footballer. What kind of player couldn't even take a penalty? But it was too late for that now, Dot was already in the goal and Edie was staring at Leah expectantly. She had no choice. Taking a deep breath, she took a few steps back and made her run-up. Her shoe connected solidly with the football and she watched miserably as it sailed through the air . . . right into Dot's hands.

Leah's shoulders sank as Dot crowed in triumph. Her cheeks burned with embarrassment. She'd missed the goal, just like she knew she would, and to make it even worse, her new friends had seen it all! Leah braced herself for the taunts she knew were coming.

But all the captain said was, 'Don't worry. We all miss sometimes. Why don't you try again, but this time, take a bigger run-up and look towards the goal, not down at your feet, when you kick the ball. Try angling your foot a little too, so you're using the side, not your toes.'

Leah nodded and set up the ball again. She thought about what Edie had said as she got ready, trying to ignore Dot's lithe form jumping around, trying to distract her. She was just about to take her run-up when a whistle blew from the sideline.

'Looks like it's time for a water break,' Edie said. 'Come on, girls. We can continue this another time.' She gave Leah and Dot a wave before jogging towards the changing room.

Leah was surprised by how disappointed she felt about their practice session being cut short. Penalties were her idea of a nightmare, but with Edie's encouragement, for the first time she'd really felt like maybe she could have scored. She hoped she got another chance at it.

'You're a really good goalkeeper, Dot,' Leah told her friend as they followed the captain across the grass.

Dot blushed. 'Thanks,' she said. 'When the team have time, they let me practise with them.'

When the two girls reached the changing room, George and Mimi were already there, lounging on the grass. Rolo was spread out next to them, his golden head nestled in a patch of dandelions. The sun was getting warmer, and George had taken off his jacket, his camera lying with it.

'How are you getting on with the kits?' Dot asked as she slumped down next to them.

'Great!' George grinned. His fingertips were stained with black ink from his markers. 'We're nearly finished!'

'Does anyone know the exact time?' Leah asked. 'We need to test the pocket watch again, soon!' Although she was desperate to get home, for the first time, Leah felt a bit sad too. If the watch did work, that would mean leaving Dot and Edie and the team behind.

'I think I heard Mary say it was quarter to twelve,' Mimi said, shading her eyes and looking up at the sun as if for confirmation.

'We should get ready, then. We don't want to—'

'Oh no,' Dot groaned, interrupting Leah. 'Not him again.'

Leah, George and Mimi turned to see what had caught Dot's attention. Leah's heart sank as she spied the skeletal outline of Mr Smelting marching across the pitch towards the changing room. This couldn't be good.

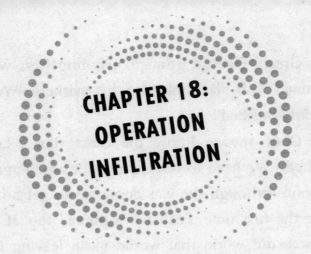

CHAPTER 18: OPERATION INFILTRATION

'I had an anonymous tip-off that I might find you all here,' Mr Smelting said, his titanic nose pointed snootily up towards the sky. 'I see that my information was correct.'

'We're not doing anything wrong, sir,' Edie said, polite but firm, but Leah couldn't help noticing that even she looked small standing in front of his looming figure.

The team were stood in a loose semi-circle behind her and Leah, Mimi, George and Dot had jogged over to join them.

'Oh, I don't doubt that, Miss Partridge,' he assured her, but his oily voice didn't sound like he believed his own words. 'Still, it would be remiss of me not to investigate these things, wouldn't it?'

'Are you satisfied with what you've seen?' Mary said sharply from behind Edie, frowning deeply.

Mr Smelting scanned them all. In the sunlight, his gaunt face made him look even more like a skeleton than ever before. Leah shuddered as his icy hooded eyes swept over her. He seemed to be enjoying their discomfort, a small curve of his lips giving away his amusement.

'Well, as you aren't operating on official FA grounds, it appears that you *are* following the rules we stipulated.' His eyes scanned the field. Littered with cones and footballs, it was clear that the ladies had been training. 'However, I can see that perhaps you are toeing a very thin line between compliance and disobedience.'

'We're just playing for enjoyment, sir,' Edie's voice was tight. 'There's nothing more to it.'

'I see. Rest assured, Miss Partridge, I will be passing my findings on to the head office.'

'That's surely not necessary,' Mary scoffed.

'Isn't it? After all, are those not football shirts behind you?' He pointed a spindly finger towards a pile of neatly folded shirts. They were the ones that George and Mimi had been working on. The top shirt showed Edie's name, 'Partridge', clearly written out across the back. 'Why ever would you need team shirts if you aren't planning to play against another team?'

Dot was speaking before anyone could stop her. 'We wouldn't need those shirts if you—'

'I think you're jumping to conclusions, Mr Smelting,' Edie spoke loudly over Dot. 'Despite your ban, the Crickle End Champions are still a football team, and football teams should have football shirts, even if they can't compete.'

'A football team?' Mr Smelting snorted. 'If I had my way, the likes of you lot wouldn't even be allowed to kick a ball, let alone form a team. Most unseemly for young ladies!'

Up until then Edie had done a good job of managing the situation, but with Mr Smelting's words the team erupted into angry noise.

'We'll do something unseemly in a minute if you're not careful, Mr Smelting,' Sarah said angrily over the noise as Lizzie shook her fist furiously in the air.

'Please!' Edie shouted desperately, trying to regain control of the team. 'Let's not lose our tempers!'

Leah watched the argument avidly – until a frantic motion out of the corner of her eye caught her attention. It was Mimi. She, George and Dot had moved away from the shouting footballers and Mimi was gesturing for Leah to join them.

'What's up?' Leah asked when she reached them. She cast a glance over her shoulder. The noise had died down slightly. It looked like Edie had managed to calm the situation. Behind her, Mr Smelting was smiling smugly, his arms crossed in satisfaction across his chest. He'd wanted to rile the players up, Leah realised. He'd done it on purpose.

'This is our chance, L,' Mimi said. 'If Mr Smelting's here, he's not at his office.'

Leah waited, not understanding. Mimi sighed and rolled her eyes. George piped up, 'He doesn't have his blue bag with him!'

Leah grinned. 'The kits! That means this would

be the perfect time to head back and see if we can find them.'

Dot nodded, determined. 'Exactly. We should go now before he notices us.' She reached into her dress pocket and pulled out a familiar folded square of paper. 'I've got Charlie's map.'

George ran back to the changing room, grabbing his jacket and his camera from the grass. 'Come on, Rolo,' he called, beckoning at the dog still lying amongst the dandelions. At the sound of his name, Rolo's flopping ears twitched and he bolted to his feet, loping after the children as they rushed across the field.

CHAPTER 19:
ROLO RIOT

Now they had Charlie's map, it was easy to find Mr Smelting's office. It was located to the west of the town, in an area where the shops had long ago given way to streets full of looming buildings. Dot brought them to a stop in front of one with a bright red door that was stood slightly ajar, as if inviting them in. There was a cluster of bushes outside, and the four of them ducked behind it, Rolo sitting by Mimi's side.

'Okay,' George whispered. 'What now? What's our plan?'

'Do we need one?' Dot asked.

'Well, we can't just go rushing in there,' said George.

'It's simple!' Mimi declared. She stood up

straight and threw her shoulders back with a flourish. 'I can just *act* my way in.' She took a decisive step forward, but Leah pulled her back down.

'Mimi! You can't just go waltzing in there and hope for the best!'

'Are you doubting my acting skills?' Mimi looked annoyed. 'Have you forgotten my stunning performance outside the train station?'

Leah rolled her eyes in exasperation. 'Of course not. But we need to be careful. We don't know who's in there and if we're caught we don't have any evidence to prove that Mr Smelting really stole the kits. We could get into loads of trouble for breaking and entering.'

'Oh,' Mimi looked crestfallen. She bit her lip, flushing slightly. 'You're right. I totally didn't think of that.' Rolo gave a whine and pawed at her hand.

'We need a proper plan,' said George firmly.

'We could just go in and ask to see what's in the bag?' Dot suggested. 'Maybe if we ask someone nicely, they'll just let us . . .' Dot trailed off as

Leah, George and Mimi stared incredulously at her. Her cheeks coloured pink. 'Yeah, you're right. That probably wouldn't work.'

Leah frowned, thoughtful. 'What we need is a distraction. Something that will let us get in and out of there without anyone seeing us.'

Suddenly, Rolo shot to his feet, letting out a loud bark that made them all jump.

'Rolo!' Mimi chastised him. 'What are you doing?'

Rolo barked again, louder this time, and then he shot around the side of the bush.

'He's heading straight for the office door!' Dot gasped.

'Rolo, come back!' Mimi called, frantic. The four of them peered over the top of the bush, watching as the little dog trotted up the front path towards the office door. He looked back at them, as if inviting them to follow him, then nosed the door open further. He disappeared inside.

'What do we do now?' Mimi cried, dismayed. 'We can't just leave him in there!'

Suddenly, there was a loud shriek from inside

the building. They heard an answering bark and then an almighty crash as if something had fallen from a great height. Another scream rang out, followed by the unmistakable sound of Rolo's yelp.

Mimi jumped to her feet, her expression distraught. 'He's hurt!' she cried, and before any of the others could stop her, she sprinted out from behind the bush and up the path, her braids flying behind her.

'Mimi, wait!' Leah called. But it was too late, Mimi had already disappeared into the office.

Leah, George and Dot exchanged a nervous glance, before all three of them rushed up the pathway. As they reached the door, Leah thought she heard Mimi shout.

George had heard it too. 'Quick!' he cried. 'We've got to get in there!'

Leah shoved the door open. They were in a short corridor, and on the carpet in front of them were the distinctive outlines of Rolo's muddy paw prints. If that wasn't enough to tell them which direction to go in, the banging and crashing at the end of the corridor was. They rushed towards it.

The room they ran into was in complete chaos. A number of filing cabinets had been tipped over and papers were strewn across the floor. Pencils littered the carpet where the pot had fallen off the large wooden desk and a mug had spilt its brown contents across the cream rug. In the centre of it all, standing upon a chair, was a small blonde woman. Her hands were clutched against her chest as she stared in terror at Rolo, who was zooming around her in crazed circles. This was not the kind of distraction Leah had been hoping for.

'Rolo! Stop!' Mimi was shouting, trying desperately to stop the dog causing any more chaos. Leah rushed to help her and together they managed to catch Rolo by the collar as he galloped past them.

'I'm so sorry!' Leah gasped. 'He's not normally like this. I don't know what's wrong with him!' Now that he'd been caught, Rolo let Mimi scoop him up into her arms where he couldn't cause any more trouble.

'Here,' George said, holding his hand up to the blonde lady. 'Let me help you down, Ms . . . ?'

'Mrs Miller,' she gasped. 'You should keep

better control of that beast!'

'We're very sorry,' Mimi said, frowning down at Rolo. He wagged his tail innocently.

'Can we help you clean up, Mrs Miller?' Dot offered, stooping down to collect a bunch of pencils. 'It's the least we can do.'

Together, they set out about restoring the office. Mrs Miller stood behind her desk, smoothing her hair and fretfully restacking her papers.

It took both Leah and George to push the fallen filing cabinets back into position. As they lifted the second one, Leah let out a little gasp. Underneath was Mr Smelting's blue bag! Once the filing cabinet was back where it belonged, Leah shot a glance over her shoulder to make sure Mrs Miller wasn't looking before she crouched down next to the bag and opened it.

Leah pushed her hand inside, feeling a surge of triumph as her fingers encountered something soft. Eagerly, she pulled it out, expecting to find a white football shirt in her hand, but instead, a knitted white and red scarf appeared.

'What?' Leah whispered. She peered inside the

hole, only to see a couple of balls of wool and two knitting needles.

'Oh, thank goodness!' Mrs Miller suddenly cried. She appeared at Leah's side. Anxiously, she took the scarf from Leah, holding it close to her face and scrutinising the weave intensely. Finally, she sighed in relief. 'I'm so pleased they're still in one piece.'

'Sorry, but what are they?' Leah asked curiously. Over Mrs Miller's shoulder, she could see that Dot was peering at them, her eyes darting between the blue bag and the scarf in Mrs Miller's hands. Leah gave her a small head shake to let her know that the kits were nowhere to be seen, and Dot's face fell.

'They're Arsenal scarves,' Mrs Miller was explaining. 'My sons are terrific fans, but the official scarves are too expensive to buy. A friend – well, my boss, actually – he has a real talent for knitting, and he made these for my boys.'

'Oh, how kind of him,' Leah said, but her voice was dull with disappointment.

'Yes, he's quite an important man in the

footballing world, actually,' Mrs Miller said, her voice bright with pride. 'Proper football, that is. Nothing like those indecent women throwing themselves around the pitch in town. Shameful.' She shook her head, her mouth twisted with distaste.

'Hey!' Dot yelped, offended.

Leah spoke over her, before Dot could say anything that might get them in trouble. 'We'd best be going, Mrs Miller. We're very sorry, once again, for all the trouble our dog caused you. We'll keep better control of him next time.'

Mrs Miller sniffed. 'Yes, you'd better.' She looked just like Mr Smelting when he tossed his nose up into the air. Leah could see why the woman liked working for him.

Rolo didn't need any convincing to leave. Mimi waved at him and he leapt to his feet, following the four of them back down the corridor and out onto the street. Despite his earlier yelp, he didn't look like he was hurt.

'So, Mr Smelting didn't take the kits then.' Dot's expression was miserable.

'No,' George agreed. 'It turns out he just really likes knitting.'

'We're right back where we started,' Dot moaned.

'Don't be sad, Dot,' Leah said, trying to sound reassuring. 'It might seem like we've gone backwards, but at least we've crossed one suspect off our list. He might not be very nice, but we know for sure that Mr Smelting isn't the thief.'

Dot nodded but she didn't say anything. Her eyes were full of disappointment and a twinge of guilt.

Leah struggled not to spiral down into the same despair. Instead, she tried to tell herself to look forward. The thief was still out there, and sooner or later they were bound to leave a clue behind that would lead the children straight to them. Still, as they walked back to the training ground, Leah couldn't help but feel that Dot was right. They were back to square one, and if they didn't figure this out soon, the watch might *never* take them home.

CHAPTER 20:
THE FINAL STRAW

The children were quiet as they made their way back to the training ground, until Dot suddenly stopped in the middle of the path. Her eyes narrowed as she stared into the distance.

'What's wrong, Dot?' Leah asked.

'It's the team. There!' Dot pointed up the road. Now that she knew what she was looking for, Leah could see the players trooping towards them. Dot frowned. 'What are they doing here? Training shouldn't be finished yet.' She broke into a jog.

As they approached, Leah could immediately see that something was wrong. That morning at the training pitch the players had all seemed lighter somehow. As if the upcoming match had lifted a weight from their shoulders. Now they were hunched over, their chins drooping down towards their chests. Anna trailed at the back, clutching the hem of her dress, behind Mary, who had her arms looped over Edie and Jo on either side. She was limping.

'What happened?' Mimi said.

'Are you okay, Mary?' Dot sounded anxious.

'It was all my fault,' Mary moaned miserably. 'I'm so sorry.'

Edie patted Mary's shoulder consolingly.

'What are you talking about?' Leah asked.

Edie heaved a great sigh. 'It's over,' she said. 'We're calling off the match.'

'What?' Dot gasped. 'Why?'

Shaking her head, Edie told them, 'Someone has stolen all of our footballs. We can't play without them.'

'Surely someone will have a football you can borrow?' George said, frowning.

'That's not the worst part, though,' Edie paused, steeling herself to deliver the news. 'The trophy has been taken, too.'

'No!' Dot's voice was filled with anguish. 'How did this happen?'

'I told you,' Mary said, sounding uncharacteristically quiet. 'It was all my fault. We'd begun to pack everything away, and on my way to the shed I stepped in a divot and tripped.

I thought I'd snapped my ankle.'

'We all rushed to help,' Edie said. 'And by the time we'd got Mary on her feet, the thief had already been and gone.'

Another theft. Leah gritted her teeth. First the shirts, and now this! And with no witnesses, there was no telling who had taken the equipment and the trophy.

'We need to go and look for clues,' she said aloud, directing the comment at no one in particular.

Edie shook her head. 'We searched the shed. There was nothing.'

Leah frowned. 'Maybe a fresh pair of eyes might–'

'I appreciate your enthusiasm, Leah,' Edie interrupted. 'But there's no point. It's over.'

Leah gaped at her. 'You can't give up this easily!'

'We don't want to,' Sarah interjected. 'But there's only so much we can take. Too many people don't want us to play this match. No matter how hard we try, we're doomed.'

Leah wanted to shout that it wasn't true, but lots of the other players were nodding along, even Mary.

'At least if we accept defeat now we can avoid the humiliation on the pitch tomorrow,' Lizzie said morosely from behind Mary's shoulder.

'But . . .' Leah's protests trailed off as she saw the resignation on every player's face.

'Go home, kids,' Mary said sadly. 'There's nothing you can do.'

Slowly, the players trudged past, Mary limping along as best she could. The children watched in silence. No one said anything until they'd turned the corner and disappeared from view.

Leah rounded on the others. 'We should get to that shed,' she told them firmly.

George, Mimi and Dot exchanged an uneasy look. Finally, Mimi said, 'What's the point, L? You heard the team. They're throwing in the towel.'

'They might be, but we can't! We can still save this football match.' Leah turned to Dot. 'If we don't do this, Dot, your dreams of becoming a

Crickle End Champion will be over! If the match is cancelled, the team might never recover! Do you want that to happen?'

Dot looked uncomfortable. 'Well, no . . . but I don't see how we can stop it.'

'Besides,' Leah went on, turning to George and Mimi, 'I've been thinking. Remember when Dot said the watch must be keeping us in the past for a reason? Well, I think it wants us to help the team pull off this football match! That means if we don't solve this, we might never be able to get back home.'

George's eyes went wide with panic, but Mimi only nodded in determination. 'We have to keep going!' she said. 'Leah's right. Let's go to the shed and see what we can find. We just need to keep calm and search for clues.'

Leah grinned wildly, her gaze swinging between her friends. 'Let's go solve this mystery!'

CHAPTER 21:
LOST IN TIME

The equipment shed was locked when they reached the training field.

Leah rattled the padlock angrily. 'Great,' she groaned. 'How're we meant to get in? Mary had said there's only one key.'

'That's true,' Dot agreed, but she was smiling. 'Luckily, I know where Edie keeps it.' She darted round the side of the changing room. Leah heard a faint banging, and then Dot reappeared, a rusty brass key clenched in her fist. She inserted it into the ancient-looking padlock and the arm sprang open with a satisfying *clunk*.

The children peered into the shed. It looked similar to earlier, but the spot where the big bag of footballs had rested was conspicuously empty.

George lifted his camera and snapped a picture of the crime scene.

'Can you see anything?' he asked.

'Not yet,' Leah replied, stepping further into the shed. Her eyes ran over the rows of cones and hoops. 'Let me just—'

'L, watch out!' Mimi grabbed Leah's arm, pulling her back. She pointed towards the floor. White paint had spread out across the boards, pooling out of the tub they'd been using to paint the pitch lines. Leah had almost stepped straight in it.

'The thief must have knocked it over when they snatched the trophy,' Leah mused.

'Look!' Mimi cried, pointing. 'That's a footprint!'

Sure enough, when Leah crouched down, she could see the outline of a shoe staining the floorboards. The edge of it was blurred and scuffed, as if someone had tried to rub it out. Leah scanned the floor, and sure enough, lying to the side was a boot brush, its dirty bristles flecked with white. 'The thief must have stepped in the paint in their rush to leave,' Leah said. 'And then tried to rub out the evidence. Unsuccessfully.'

'Well, at least we know that it's not anyone on the football team,' Dot said. She sounded relieved.

'How do you know that?' George asked curiously.

'Look at the print,' Dot told him. 'There aren't any stud marks. If it had been a footballer, you'd have been able to see the studs on their boots in the footprint. That one is completely smooth.'

'Okay, so we know that someone from outside the team is trying to sabotage them. We know it's not Mr Smelting, but it could be someone else who doesn't want the ladies' team to succeed,' Mimi said thoughtfully. She slammed her fist into her palm. 'If only I'd thought to bring some sticky tape. I could have searched for fingerprints.'

George rolled his eyes. 'You watch too much TV, Mimi,' he sighed, exasperated. 'That stuff doesn't actually work in real life.'

'Yes, it does!' Mimi was outraged.

'What's teevee?' Dot asked quizzically.

Mimi gaped, appalled. 'You don't have TV yet?' she spluttered. 'I feel sorry for you, Dot. I couldn't live without it. It's like a box that contains all the stories in the world—'

'Guys,' Leah interrupted. 'Focus! We don't have much time.'

'And if we don't solve the case,' George lamented, 'the pocket watch won't work and we won't be able to get home.' He reached into his pocket, groping for the watch's chain.

'We just need time to think,' Leah tried to reassure them.

Suddenly, George gave a loud gasp. His eyes were wide. 'No!' he shouted.

'What?' Leah said in alarm.

'The watch! It's gone!'

'How is that possible?' Mimi cried. 'It's been in

your pocket this whole time! You haven't taken off your jacket, have you?'

'No!' George babbled, and then he paused. 'Oh no. Well . . . actually . . .'

'George,' Leah moaned, dropping her head into her hands.

'It was only for a little while earlier when we were sitting on the grass!' George mewled. 'I was so warm and I just took my coat off for a minute!'

'Was the watch there when you put your jacket back on?' Mimi asked urgently.

'Yes! Actually . . . no? Maybe? I don't know!' George's voice quivered.

'Someone must have *taken* it.' Leah frowned. 'I bet the same person who stole the footballs and the trophy also stole our watch.'

'Even if that's true, it still doesn't help us get home, L,' Mimi said sadly.

Leah nodded in agreement. 'You're right. But what it does mean is that we *really* need to find this thief. Otherwise . . .' she gulped. 'Otherwise, we'll be stuck in the past *forever*.'

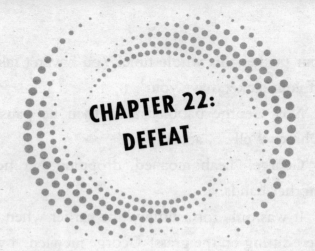

CHAPTER 22:
DEFEAT

The children trudged back to Dot's house for the night. The sun was fading fast, and Leah wasn't in the mood for another night-time excursion.

She was relieved when the comforting sight of red-brick terraces appeared. She was craving the warmth of Dot's cosy living-room fire and the comfort of her mum's delicious cooking. As they got closer to the front door, however, a familiar figure came into view.

It was Anna. She was lingering at the bottom of Dot's path, nervously dragging the toe of her white plimsoll across the pavement. Her already pale skin had gone pallid, her red hair stark against her white cheeks. The only exception was her hands, both of which looked pink and a little sore as they clutched at the hem of her dress. Leah supposed that wasn't unusual, though, when your mother was a washerwoman. She could imagine that when Anna wasn't helping the football team, she'd often be roped into laundry duty with her mum.

'Hi, Anna,' Dot said, her voice glum. 'What's up?'

Anna licked her lips. She opened her mouth as if to speak, but then shut it again. Her feet shifted against the ground.

Leah frowned, exchanging a concerned glance with Mimi and George. 'Is everything okay, Anna?'

Again, Anna started to speak, her lips forming shapes, but no words came out.

'Are you in trouble?' George asked.

'We can help if you are,' Leah reassured her. She glanced at Mimi for backup, but her friend was frowning at the floor. Leah started forward, her hand outstretched towards Anna, but the older girl stepped back quickly, shaking her head. Rolo whined.

'No,' she said finally, her voice barely audible. 'I'm not in trouble, but . . .'

'But . . .?' Leah encouraged her.

Anna's lower lip trembled, and her cerulean eyes shifted, focusing intently on the pavement below her shuffling feet. 'I think–'

'Dot!'

The shout made Anna jump, her soft words dying immediately. The children turned their heads towards Dot's house. Her mother was standing in the doorway, hands perched on her hips and a fierce frown marring her usually friendly face.

'Where on God's green earth have you been?' she demanded. 'I've not seen hide nor hair of you since you all raced off this morning.'

Dot looked chagrined. 'Sorry, Ma,' she apologised. 'We've been with the team. It's training day.'

'I don't care if it's the day of the second coming, you know that when that sun goes down, you're to be home!'

'It was an accident . . .'

Mrs Andrews's frown grew even deeper. 'And I told you last night that it was an accident you'd best have no plans of repeating, but here we are.' She pointed a stern finger into the house. 'Get inside, all of you. I've spent all afternoon cooking your dinner and I'll not see it ruined because you don't know how to tell the time.'

Dot groaned. 'Sorry, Anna, we've got to go.'

'But—' Anna's protests died as Dot started to trudge up the path, cringing under her mother's disapproving sigh.

Leah shrugged apologetically. 'We'll talk tomorrow,' she told Anna. 'Just remember, though, if you are in trouble, we can help you.'

Mimi and George also said their goodbyes, following Leah up the path and through the front door. In the kitchen, Leah could hear Dot's mother talking about Rolo, who had trotted into the house after Dot.

'Don't worry, I'll put him in the garden,' Dot replied, and then there was the sound of a door opening and closing as poor Rolo was expelled into the backyard.

Dinner was a quiet affair. As soon as the plates hit the table, Dot's brothers seemed to materialise from thin air, slipping into their seats and attacking their food with impressive vigour. Leah picked at her chicken and potatoes. Her appetite seemed to have disintegrated. It was bad enough that they had no leads on the thief, but now their only way home had been stolen too. Her lip trembled as she thought about her mum and dad, waiting for her. If they didn't find the watch, she'd never see them again!

'Well,' Mrs Andrews announced, once they were all finished. She began to collect their plates. 'Training day has certainly tuckered you all out. Why don't you head on up to bed?'

'Ma, it's Dot's turn to do the dishes,' Charlie chirped.

'Well, she won't have to now that you've volunteered, will she?'

'Ma!' Charlie whined. 'That's not fair!'

'Oh, hush,' Mrs Andrews's eyes lingered on her silent daughter. She looked concerned. 'Dot can do two days of dishes next week.'

Dot led Leah, Mimi and George upstairs to her room. Once inside, she lit a candle and then slumped down onto the bed. George and Mimi settled themselves cross-legged on the floor.

'I hope Anna's okay,' Leah said, joining Dot. 'She looked really upset earlier.'

Dot shrugged. 'It's hard to know with Anna. She's so quiet. I'm sure she's fine though.'

'We can ask her tomorrow,' Mimi said, but she sounded distracted. When Leah glanced at her, she saw that her best friend was gazing blankly at Dot's bedroom wall.

'What's going on, Mimi?' Leah asked.

Mimi jumped, snapping out of her trance. Her eyes refocused and she gave a rueful smile. 'Sorry,' she said. 'I've just been thinking . . . there's something about that footprint we found in the shed that's been bothering me. Something familiar.'

Leah sat upright. 'Yeah?' she said eagerly, but Mimi shook her head, her nose twitching in frustration.

'That's the thing, though. I can't figure out

what it is. I just can't put my finger on it.'

Leah slumped back onto her elbows, disappointed. Normally, in books and movies, the detectives always seemed to know how the clues fit together, then they'd find one big breakthrough clue and the villain would be caught. But their clues were all in a tangle, and there was no breakthrough in sight. They were going to be stuck here forever.

Almost as if George sensed Leah's thoughts shifting towards the pocket watch, he gave a dispirited sigh. 'We've been in the past for almost two days now.' He paused and then added in a wobbly voice, 'I miss home.'

'Me too,' Leah admitted miserably. She imagined what her mum would be doing now. Probably sitting on the sofa with a hot cup of coffee, getting ready to watch some of the trashy programmes they liked. Usually, Leah would be curled up right next to her with a steaming mug of hot chocolate. Then her dad would walk through the door and loudly complain about the rubbish they were watching, although they all knew he enjoyed it too. He'd get his own drink, and the three of them would settle in together. The thought of them sitting at home without her made Leah's chest ache.

'Hey,' Mimi suddenly said. 'If we've been here two days, that means tomorrow is the big game against Westfield High.'

'Oh man!' Leah groaned. 'I totally forgot about that.'

'It's meant to be your debut as our top penalty taker,' Mimi pointed out.

Leah sighed. 'Not anymore,' she said quietly.

'I guess I won't get any of my photos featured in the local newspaper, either,' George lamented.

Dot suddenly sat upright. 'I know this isn't ideal,' she said, 'but at least we're all here together. And we've sort of had a good time, haven't we?' On the last sentence, her voice quivered, as if she wasn't sure of their answer.

Leah took her hand, squeezing it with her own. 'Of course, Dot. We're so lucky to have met you. It's just . . .' she looked at Mimi and George. 'This isn't our home. We've got to get back.'

'Well, if we find the thief, we'll find your watch, too,' Dot pointed out.

Leah rubbed her forehead. 'I know that, but we've got no leads! We're at a dead end.' Saying it out loud was worse than just thinking it. It was like she was finally admitting defeat. She curled her hands into fists.

'We were so close to pulling it off,' Mimi said quietly. 'The final would have gone ahead and we would have accomplished what the watch sent us here to do. Even if we do find it now, it'll be too late, anyway. There's no way the team will be able to play tomorrow. We've failed.'

'It's not over yet!' Dot protested. 'There's still time. We can find a ball from somewhere, and we have the kits that George and Mimi worked on.'

Leah wasn't convinced. 'What about the trophy?' She shook her head. 'It's no use, Dot. The match is a lost cause.'

Dot was silent, but then she frowned, her cheeks turning an angry pink. 'A lost cause?' she repeated. 'So you really are just going to give up then. Even though you said earlier that we could work this out. You don't believe in the team enough to help them.'

'Dot!' Mimi exclaimed, appalled. 'That's not true!'

Dot suddenly stood up from the bed, her movements stiff and jerky. 'All you care about is leaving! I can't believe I thought you'd be able to help.'

'And all you care about is your stupid football match!' Leah retorted furiously. 'We've done our best, Dot, but we're running out of time. We've got more important things to worry about now. I'm sorry we couldn't save the match, but we need to focus on getting home.'

As soon as the words were out of her mouth, Leah wished she could stuff them back in. But it was too late. Dot's eyes narrowed.

'Like I said, you don't care about the team at all. I should never have trusted you,' she seethed, turning away from them.

Leah squeezed her eyes shut. She'd been so focused on the watch that now she'd lost her temper and made everything worse.

'Dot,' she sighed apologetically. 'I'm sorry, I didn't mean those things I said.'

But Dot wasn't listening, and she refused to speak to any of them. Her back was rigid as she changed into her pyjamas and got into bed. When Leah and Mimi slipped under the covers next to her, she rolled over so that she was facing the wall.

Leah groaned and rubbed at her eyes. Things seemed to be going from bad to worse.

CHAPTER 23:
AN ANONYMOUS
TIP-OFF

A loud banging shattered the early morning silence. Leah sat bolt upright, her hair in disarray, as she tried to work out where she was and what was going on.

'Alright, alright!' came a deep voice from outside on the landing. Leah guessed it must be Dot's dad. They hadn't had a chance to meet him yet. She listened as his footsteps thumped down the stairs. The front door creaked as it opened and there was a mumble as he greeted whoever was at the door.

Next to her, Mimi and Dot were stirring, and on the floor George sat upright in his nest of blankets.

'What's going on?' Mimi groaned. She sat up

and stretched her arms above her head as she yawned.

'Someone's at the door,' Leah answered.

'Ugh,' George moaned. 'Can we go back to sleep?'

'Dot!' The deep voice called up the stairs. 'Can you come down here, please?'

Dot rubbed at her eyes. 'Just a minute!' She called sleepily. Without saying a word to the others, she clambered over them and disappeared onto the landing. Once she was gone, Leah scrambled out of bed too. She hovered by the open door, listening.

Leah could hear Dot's father talking to her at the top of the stairs. 'I know football is important to you, but it's half past seven in the morning! It's much too early for Edie to be calling,' he rumbled.

Edie? Edie was at the front door?

'Come on,' Leah said, urging George and Mimi up.

Still in their nightclothes, they crept out of the bedroom and down the stairs, stepping lightly so they didn't make too much noise. When they reached the living room, Dot was just opening the front door.

'Hi, Edie,' she greeted the captain, confused. 'What are you doing here?'

Edie's expression was sombre, and her usually chaotic black curls were pulled back into a severe bun. Her dark eyes were serious. Behind her, the dawn-tinged sky still held smudges of night, the sun not yet strong enough to fully chase them away.

'I'm sorry about the early hour, Dot, but I had to come. I received an anonymous tip-off.'

Leah frowned as she crowded in behind Dot. *An anonymous tip-off? Hadn't Mr Smelting also received an anonymous tip-off yesterday?*

'About what?' Dot's confusion deepened.

Edie looked uncomfortable, as if she didn't want to say the next words, but she forced them out. 'About our missing equipment and the trophy. The informant said they were here. In your shed.'

Dot's jaw dropped and she stared at Edie in shock. Her face had turned a frightening milky white. 'Here?' she squeaked. 'Why would they be here?'

'I don't know the answer to that,' Edie said, her mouth a tight line. 'Look, I know it's probably all false, but I need to check it out. What kind of captain would I be if I didn't?'

'Edie, I swear to you, I don't have the equipment or the trophy,' Dot said earnestly, her brown eyes wide. 'I would never take those things.'

'You won't mind me taking a look in the shed, then?' Edie asked, her head tilted to the side.

'Of course, not,' Dot spluttered. 'Please, come in.'

She ushered the captain into the house and out of the back door into the garden. Leah, Mimi and George exchanged a disbelieving look and followed after them. Leah shivered as they stepped outside. It was cold this early in the morning, and a fine layer of frost coated everything like a lace shawl. As they all stepped into the garden, Rolo got to his feet. He'd been lying by the fence at the end of the yard, and now he barked loudly, pawing at the wood. Mimi shushed him. His barks dwindled to disappointed whines.

'I'm sorry someone's leading you on a wild goose chase,' Dot was saying as she fished underneath a flowerpot for the key to the shed. She found it and slotted it into the lock. 'Maybe it's their idea of a joke.'

'Well,' Edie said, 'I'll just have a quick look around and be on my way. If I ever find the person who thinks it's funny to spread such lies, I'll have a few choice words for them.'

Dot gave a small laugh. Her teeth were chattering in the cold. She turned the key and pulled the shed door wide open so that Edie could peer inside and see for herself that the stolen equipment and trophy were not there.

Except, when the door swung open the shed was not as empty as Dot had expected it to be. She gave a horrified gasp. Leah, Mimi and George surged forward, peering over her shoulder to see for themselves. Leah felt her stomach sink.

'Oh, Dot,' Edie said sadly, shaking her head.

Inside the gloomy shed was the unmistakable shape of the team's lumpy football bag. On the floor next to it, stacked neatly, were the lucky kits that Dot had picked up from Mrs Matthews's house just the other day. Most importantly, though, was the unmistakable flash of gold they all saw buried amongst the gardening equipment in the wheelbarrow. Edie strode forward, plunging her hands into the collection of tools. She gave a tug, and then the burnished face of the Women's Championship Cup trophy was revealed, winking accusingly in the frosty morning light.

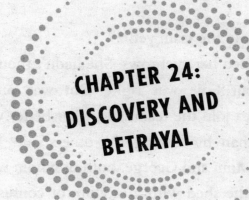

CHAPTER 24: DISCOVERY AND BETRAYAL

'Dot, how could you do something like this?' Edie's quiet words splintered the shocked silence.

'But – but – I didn't!' Dot's brown eyes welled with unshed tears as she stared in dismay at the contents of the shed.

Edie's scowl was thunderous. 'There's no point lying to me now. Not when the proof is right before my eyes. First the ban, and now this!'

'Edie, I swear, it wasn't me! Why would I take them? It would destroy the team!'

Edie threw her hands into the air. 'I don't know what you hoped to achieve, Dot. Maybe you wanted to destroy the team. Were you hoping that some of the players would leave, opening a spot for you to jump into? You know you're too young to join the team yet!'

Leah raised her eyebrows. She hadn't thought of that, but Edie was right, Dot was pretty desperate to join the team, and what better way to do it than by forcing the others out? She looked at Mimi and George, both of whom were staring at the shed with a mixture of confusion and surprise.

But Dot was shaking her head furiously, strands of dark hair slicing the air. 'I would *never* do that. I know I'm not old enough. I'm happy to wait! All I want is for the team to win and do well.'

Edie shrugged and sighed. 'It's hard for me to believe you now, especially after what I've seen this morning.' She gestured into the shed, the trophy clutched in her hand, motioning at the balls and shirts. All proof of Dot's betrayal.

The sadness in Dot's eyes suddenly hardened, turning to a white-hot anger. She balled her fists at her side and stamped one slippered foot. 'I'm being framed,' she declared. 'Someone is trying to make out that this is my fault.'

Edie gave a bark of laughter, but there wasn't any joy in it. It sounded empty. 'Who would possibly be trying to frame you? No one has time for that, Dot. We're all adults with busy lives.'

As quick as it came, the anger drained from Dot's face and she stared up at Edie mournfully. 'Why won't you believe me?' A single tear slipped down her cheek.

Edie sighed. 'Because, as much as I want to, there are too many coincidences for me to ignore. Out of everyone on the team, it would have been easiest for you to steal the trophy and equipment.' She held up her hand, ticking her points off on her fingers as she spoke. 'For one thing, you collect the kits from the laundry every week. And when the balls went missing, where were you? You know where the key is and where everything is kept. Plus, you're obsessed with that trophy, Dot. You can't deny it. We've all seen how you look at it, and only yesterday you said you'd been dreaming of taking it home.'

'Yeah, but only after winning it!' Dot protested indignantly. 'I didn't mean I'd *steal* it.'

But Edie was shaking her head, deaf to Dot's words. 'I just wish you'd tell me why. You've got

so much talent. You know I'd have you as our goalkeeper in a heartbeat. You just needed to have a little patience.'

'Edie,' Dot pleaded, her hands clasped tightly in front of her. 'You've got to believe me. I didn't do it!'

Sadness lined the captain's features as she looked at Dot one last time, and then turned her face away. Silently, she stepped into the shed, looping the bag of balls over her shoulder and scooping up the kits into her arms along with the trophy. Dot watched helplessly from the garden, her arms wrapped tight around her torso.

As Edie stepped back outside, she stopped, looking down at Dot one last time. Her expression was sad, a regretful frown pinching her brow. 'Don't come to the match today. You won't be welcome. In fact, it's best if you just don't come back to training at all.' Her voice was mournful. 'We can't trust you. And I would never allow anyone I don't trust to be part of my team.'

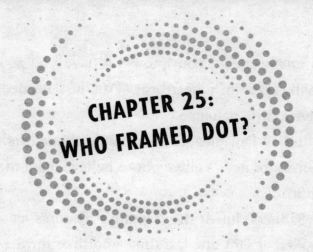

CHAPTER 25:
WHO FRAMED DOT?

The low moan that seeped out of Dot's mouth twisted Leah's heart. She didn't need to see her friend's face to know that her devastation would be clear in her expression.

Dot was slumped by the garden door, her hand braced against the wall for support.

'Did you do it?' The words were out of Leah's mouth before she could stop them. Next to her, Mimi and George crowded closer, as if they too wanted to hear Dot's answer.

Dot turned towards Leah, her expression horrified. 'How can you ask me that? Of course I didn't! Is that really what you think of me?'

Mimi bit her lip. 'Everything Edie said made sense, Dot. And all the stolen stuff *was* in your shed.'

Furious, Dot stamped her foot once more. 'I would never sabotage the team like that. They're my family. Besides, we've been together the whole time. But if you don't believe me you can all just get out of my house – right now!'

Leah shook her head. 'It's okay. If you say you didn't do it, we believe you.'

Dot twisted her nose. 'How generous of you,' she spat angrily. 'I don't see why you three care anyway. All of this started when you arrived. For all I know, *you* stole the equipment and hid it in the shed when I wasn't looking!'

Dumbstruck, Leah and Mimi glanced at each other.

'Why would we want to steal from the team?' Mimi asked, raising an eyebrow.

Dot threw her hands up. 'How would I know? We barely know each other.'

'Hey!' George's impatient voice cut across them. He had wandered away and was now standing by Rolo, in front of the fence. As they watched, Rolo stretched out his paw and clawed anxiously at the wood. 'If you'd just take a minute and stop shouting at each other, I've got something you might want to see.'

Leah and Mimi jogged over to where George was standing. Dot trudged grumpily behind them. 'What is it, George?' Leah asked.

'There,' George answered, pointing towards the gate. 'It's white paint.'

Leah inhaled sharply as she saw that George was right. Staining the edge of the panelling was a splotch of white paint. It looked as if someone covered in the stuff had clutched at the side of the gate on their way in – or out – of the garden.

'That matches the white paint spilt in the equipment shed,' Mimi said thoughtfully, leaning forward. 'Someone's been in and out of this gate recently. I'd guess it was whilst we were down at the training pitch, looking for clues. They must have snuck in here and planted the stolen items in the shed. Which means . . .'

'That someone really is trying to frame Dot,' Leah said grimly.

'I could have told you that,' Dot puffed from

beside them, but her expression was less angry than before.

Suddenly, Mimi gave an explosive gasp, her hands flying to her mouth and her eyes going wide. 'It all makes sense now!' she cried. Then she frowned, confusion twisting her mouth. 'Well, at least, some of it does . . .'

'What are you talking about?' George asked.

'I know who spilt the paint in the shed,' Mimi announced proudly. The other three crowded closer as she told them her suspicions.

George looked dubious. 'Are you sure?' he asked. 'We all know how you like jumping to conclusions . . .'

'Of course, I'm sure,' Mimi replied snippily. 'The evidence is right there.'

Leah was quiet. Mimi's words were running through her head. Could she possibly be right? It seemed so unlikely . . . but then a snippet of conversation from yesterday drifted through Leah's memory. She felt the pieces snapping into place like a tricky puzzle finally conquered.

'Mimi, you *are* right!' Leah crowed, throwing

her hands up in excitement. 'George, give me your photos!'

Bemused, George handed them over. Leah flipped through them until she reached the one she was after. The photo of the stadium stared up at her. It was the picture George had taken just before the kits were stolen. There was Mr Smelting, leaning up against the wall, the blue bag slumped at his feet. They'd been so distracted by him, they'd failed to notice all the other people in the photo. Leah's eyes scanned across them until she found what she was looking for. She'd expected to feel a surge of triumph, but instead her stomach gave a painful squeeze of disappointment.

'Look,' she said, turning the photo towards the others. They crowded in, and Dot's eyes went wide with disbelief as she saw what Leah was pointing at.

'Oh dear,' she whispered softly.

'We've got to get to Edie,' Leah said. 'She needs to know there's a thief on her team.'

CHAPTER 26:
A THIEF
AMONG US

Streets whizzed by in a frantic blur as Leah, Dot, Mimi, George and Rolo sprinted towards the training ground. They didn't have much time; the match would be starting soon!

As they got closer to the pitch, though, they were forced to slow down in order to dodge around all the people heading in the same direction. Eventually the throng became so dense that they had to abandon their jog altogether, instead dipping and diving to find a way through the busy crowd.

'You don't think all of these people are heading to the football match, do you?' Leah shouted over her shoulder.

'I hope so!' Dot called. 'The officials will have

to take notice of us if we receive this much support from the locals!'

After much pushing and shoving, they finally reached the field, where a steady stream of spectators were jostling for the best positions. The children didn't linger; they skirted the perimeter of the pitch and headed straight for the changing room.

At the door, Dot paused, her fingers clenched tightly in front of her chest.

'Don't worry,' Leah reassured her. 'You can do this.'

Dot shot her a grateful grin and then quickly pushed the door open before she could change her mind.

Inside, a sombre mood hung in the air. The team were slumped over on the benches, all of them wearing their lucky shirts. On the pegs behind them were the shirts that George and Mimi had helped to create, dangling forlornly. Leah had expected everyone to be jubilant at the return of their equipment and the trophy, which gleamed brightly on the table at the front of the

room, but instead their expressions were grim.

'What do you think you're doing?' demanded an angry voice. It was Edie, her usually kind face drawn into a frown. 'I told you not to bother coming. You aren't welcome.'

Dot drew herself up tall, mustering her courage. 'We had no choice. I told you earlier that I didn't steal the trophy or the equipment, but you wouldn't listen. Well, now you're going to have to because I know who *really* did it and they're in this room!'

The players had straightened up to listen when Dot began to talk, but with her last statement their eyes gleamed and they looked at each other suspiciously.

There was a derisive snort as Mary stood up from the bench, her arms crossed imperiously across her chest. 'Please,' she huffed. 'This is ridiculous. You're wasting our time. We know you did it. Stop making up lies to save your own skin.'

Outraged, the children began to talk over each other all at once.

'Hey!' Leah cried.

'We're not lying,' Mimi argued.

'We've got proof!' George said.

'Stop!' Edie's bellow cut across the racket. A silence fell, and Leah and her friends exchanged sheepish glances. Edie sighed, rubbing her forehead as if she were getting a headache. 'Look, you've got thirty seconds to say what you came to say and then you need to leave. We've got a match to prepare for.'

'Edie, you can't really believe these children are telling the truth,' Mary spluttered. But Edie only shrugged wearily.

'I guess we'll soon find out, won't we? At the very least, we've got to hear them out.' She gestured for Dot to speak. The changing room was suddenly very quiet as all the players turned their attention to her.

Pink spots appeared on her cheeks and she coughed awkwardly. 'Um . . .' she trailed off. Mary sighed but fell silent when Edie glared at her.

Leah grabbed Dot's hand, and when her friend

turned towards her she smiled. 'It's okay,' she told her. 'You've got this.'

Dot nodded and, taking a deep breath, she turned back to the team that she desperately wanted to be a part of. 'Earlier, we found all of the stolen equipment and the trophy hidden in my garden shed. But the thing is, I didn't put them there. Someone tried really hard to make it look like I was responsible in order to dodge the blame.' Dot squeezed her eyes shut briefly, but then she opened them and looked at every member of the team, willing them to believe her. 'That person was Mary Matthews.'

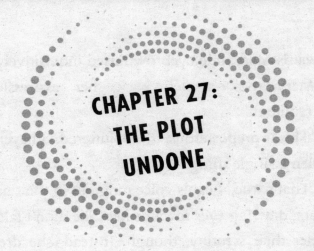

CHAPTER 27: THE PLOT UNDONE

Mary let out an ugly peal of laughter, complete with disbelieving snorts.

'You can't be serious!' she exclaimed, shaking her head. 'See, Edie, they're just trying to save themselves.'

But Edie wasn't looking at Mary. Instead, she was staring intently at Dot. 'You've made false accusations before, Dot, and this is a big one. Are you certain about this?'

'Edie, you can't really believe this–' Mary's eyes were wide.

'Be quiet, Mary,' Edie said firmly, never taking her eyes off Dot.

'I'm sure,' Dot replied quietly. Edie stared at her for a moment longer and then she turned towards Mary, one eyebrow raised inquisitively.

Mary took a step back, her expression incredulous.

'This is preposterous!' she spluttered. 'I haven't stolen a single thing!'

'That's true,' Leah's voice rang out in the small room, drawing eyes towards her. She didn't falter under their scrutiny, though. Instead, she drew her shoulders up, looking directly at Mary, whose expression had turned triumphant in response to Leah's declaration. 'You haven't stolen anything yourself. You've made Anna do it all for you.'

A low rumble like thunder rolled around the changing room as the players shifted their attention to Anna. She was cloistered at the back of the room, behind Mary, buried so deep into the shadowy corner that Leah had almost missed her when they'd first entered. With so many eyes on her, she shrank back even further, her pale cheeks flushed pink.

'At first,' Leah explained, stepping forward, 'we thought it might be one of the players. After all, the thief had to have access to the stadium changing room, as well as the equipment shed. But the footprint changed everything. When the thief stole the footballs they spilt the bucket of white paint, accidentally stepping in it and leaving a footprint. The print was smooth, without any football studs, so we knew a player couldn't be responsible. The only other people who have regular access to the shed but don't wear football boots are Dot and Anna.' Leah swivelled, looking towards Anna's hunched form. 'We knew it couldn't be Dot, but we also didn't think it could be you, Anna. At least not until we saw you later. You were holding the hem of your dress, and Mimi noticed that it was marked with flecks of white paint.'

'You tried to clean up the mess you made, but it only got worse,' Dot said. 'That's why you changed your shoes. At football training yesterday, you were wearing lace-up boots like mine, but when you came to my house last night, you'd changed into a clean pair of plimsolls because your shoes were all covered in paint.'

'That's not to mention your hands,' Leah

interjected, pointing to where Anna had her fingers laced tightly together. 'They looked sore and red because you'd spent ages scrubbing the white paint from your palms.' Anna gave a jolt and shoved her hands behind her back.

'Excuse me,' Mary abruptly interrupted, her hands on her hips. 'This so-called evidence you've presented, it doesn't have anything to do with me. Yes, it might incriminate my sister as a thief, but if it does, she acted on her own.'

Over Mary's shoulder, Leah saw hurt flash across Anna's face.

'It might look that way, Mary,' Mimi said, 'but Anna doesn't have the muscles to lug that big bag of footballs *and* the trophy out of the shed without the team seeing her. She's not fast enough.'

'She needed a distraction,' George agreed. 'And there's where you came in. You pretended to hurt your ankle, directing the team's attention while Anna smuggled out the equipment. You gave her more time.'

Edie flashed a speculative look at Mary's ankle. 'Your foot did seem to get better quite quickly,' the captain mused. Discomfort shone on Mary's face, and she refused to meet Edie's eyes.

'That's not all, though,' Leah added. 'Anna would never have been able to get all of the stolen equipment into Dot's shed without help. Plus, Rolo was in the garden. She'd have needed someone to distract him, so you worked together.'

'And you tried to warn us,' Dot said to Anna, her voice softening. 'That's what you came to tell us yesterday, wasn't it?'

Anna's bottom lip trembled and she closed her eyes.

'If all of that wasn't enough,' George said, producing his stack of photos with a flourish, 'we have evidence that places you at the stadium, just before the lucky kits were stolen.' He slipped a picture from the stack and handed it to Edie. She squinted as she scrutinised it.

'We were so focused on finding Mr Smelting that we didn't notice Mary and Anna in the bottom right-hand corner.' Mimi leaned forward and pointed them out, their distinctive red hair instantly recognisable.

In the corner Anna burst into tears, her wails overpowering Mary's weak protests.

'I'm . . . I'm . . . I'm sorry!' she snivelled. 'It all just got so out of control! Mary m . . . m . . . made me and I tried to w . . . warn you when she planned to plant the stolen equipment in your shed, but . . . I was too scared!' She dropped her head into her hands, her shoulders heaving with sobs.

Dot rushed to her side, rubbing her back comfortingly. 'Don't cry, Anna. It's okay.

None of this is your fault.'

With her hands on her hips, Edie rounded on Mary, asking her the same thing she'd asked Dot that very morning, 'Why would you do this, Mary? You're our star player and the team is your family!'

Finally, all friendliness dropped from Mary's face. She raised her eyebrows in furious disbelief. 'Family?' she exclaimed, disgust coating her voice. 'Family wouldn't do the things you've done! You deserved it after the way you've treated my sister. You've destroyed her dreams!'

Edie's brow creased in confusion. 'What are you talking about?'

Mary snorted. 'Don't pretend like you don't know. You rejected Anna when she applied to join the team last year! You told her she wasn't good enough to play and then you humiliated her further, shoving her into the background and forcing her to scrub your muddy boots and wash your filthy kits! It's demeaning and pathetic!'

'And what about me?' Dot challenged her, staring straight into Mary's cold eyes. 'Why frame me for it all? What did I do?'

'It's nothing personal, Dot,' Mary's haughty voice was slightly apologetic as she shrugged. 'You were simply the most likely culprit. You're always nosing around at the stadium and you know where the key to the shed is. It had to be you.'

'But surely stealing the equipment would have punished the whole team?' Leah blinked, bewildered.

Mary rolled her eyes. 'I was always going to return the stuff before the big game, you idiot. I just wanted Edie to feel as hopeless as Anna did when she crushed her dreams.'

Throughout Mary's tirade, Edie had said nothing, her face stoic as she listened, but now she held up her hand, a puzzled expression on her face. 'Mary,' she said, shaking her head. 'I think you've jumped to the wrong conclusions here.'

'Ha!' Mary barked. 'Of course you'd say that.'

Leah was frowning too. She could understand that sisterly love might motivate Mary to take drastic action, but . . . 'Something doesn't add up,' she said, thinking aloud. 'Why would you do all of this for Anna when she doesn't even want to be a footballer?'

A shocked silence met Leah's words, and Mary's blue eyes bulged in her face. 'What did you say?' she hissed.

Steeling herself against Mary's anger, Leah turned to Anna. 'That's right, isn't it, Anna? You've never wanted to be a footballer. You almost told me at football training yesterday, but then Edie called me away and we never got to finish our conversation.'

Anna's face crumpled, and she looked like she might dissolve into tears again. Then she took a deep breath, gathering her courage to say, 'It's true.'

'Anna!' Mary's face was a mask of shock as she stared down at her sister. 'What are you talking about? You've always wanted to be a footballer!'

But Anna was shaking her head, dashing her tears away with bunched fists.

'No, Mary, football has always been *your*

dream. I've tried to tell you but you never listen. You've always been so good at it and I could see that you were desperate for me to follow in your footsteps. I . . . I didn't want to disappoint you.'

'When Anna came for her trial,' Edie said, stepping closer to where Anna and Dot were slumped, 'she told me all of this. I tried to convince her to give it a go, because I suspected she'd have just as much talent as you, Mary, but she was adamant. She didn't want to be on the team. I thought you knew.'

Mary looked as if she'd received a thump on the head. For once, she had nothing to say.

Anna, however, seemed to have found her voice. 'I enjoy watching football, but it's not what I want to do with my life.'

As if Anna's words had woken her from an unpleasant dream, Mary wrinkled her nose. 'What do you want to do then?' It was clear from her expression that she thought anything her sister might say would never be as good as football.

Anna smiled broadly, and it was the biggest grin Leah had seen on her face since they'd first met. She puffed up her chest and said proudly, 'I want to be a doctor.'

'Ha, right!' Mary wheezed an incredulous laugh. 'That's never going to happen. Women don't become doctors. It's not proper.'

At Mary's words, the players surged to their feet, anger displayed on their faces.

'Who sounds like a government official now?' Sarah shouted.

'I bet you and that Mr Smelting would get along,' Lizzie snapped. She turned to Anna. 'Don't listen to anything she says. Women can do anything that men can, and we can do it just as well, too!'

'If not better!' Jo added, and the team laughed.

'Anyone should be allowed to do what they love,' Mimi declared, hands on her hips, and the players around her nodded.

Suddenly, Leah realised that in her confession Mary hadn't mentioned the pocket watch. She had to have it hidden away somewhere. The match was due to kick off, and that meant that noon was only a few hours away. They needed to get that watch back! She stepped forward, opening her mouth to demand that she return it . . . when the shrill sound of a whistle cut the air.

The team whirled towards the doorway where a grey-haired woman in a referee's uniform was standing, her expression bemused and a bit harried. 'I've got no idea what's going on in here, but you're causing a right racket and your opponents are ready to start. If you don't get a move on, I'll have to award them the victory by default. So, are you ready?'

'Sorry, Ref,' Edie apologised. 'We'll be out in a moment.'

The referee raised her eyebrow sceptically, but she turned and left anyway.

Edie blew her breath out in a big stream, running her hand over her head. 'Blimey, what a day this has been.' She turned to Mary, her expression angry. 'You . . . you're on the bench. I'll deal with you later. But as for you, Dot, Leah, George and Mimi,' she spread out her hands, 'I can't apologise enough. I'm sorry. I should have believed you from the beginning. I'm ashamed of how I've acted.'

Dot tilted one of her shoulders up. 'It's okay, Edie. I forgive you.'

Leah smiled at the captain, recalling what she'd said to her when Dot had saved her penalty in the training session. 'We all miss sometimes.'

Edie gave her a broad grin in return.

'Uh, guys,' Mimi suddenly interrupted. She poked her head out of the door, and then back in again. 'That referee is getting pretty angry. I think we should head outside.'

Edie nodded, her gaze sweeping across the team. 'You're right. Come on, ladies. We've got a championship to win.'

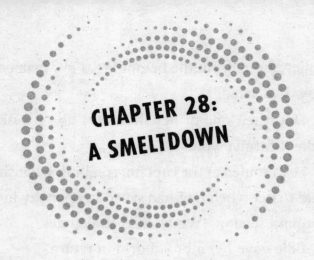

CHAPTER 28:
A SMELTDOWN

'Look at all these people!' Sarah gasped as the team filed out of the dressing room and onto the pitch. 'I can't believe it!'

The field was filled to bursting with spectators. There weren't any official stands, but someone had placed cones around the perimeter of the pitch and the crowds stood behind them, jostling each other to get a glimpse of the Crickle End Champions as they emerged from the dressing room.

It wasn't all just home supporters, either. There were plenty of black and white shirts clustered about too, worn by Whitebridge fans who had made the journey last-minute to support their team. Leah looked towards the northern edge of the grass where a small ticketing table had been set up. There was a queue of people still waiting to get in, money clutched between their fingers. Leah couldn't help the grin that spread across her face. If everyone had made a donation, the team would have more than enough money to buy all the new equipment they needed. They might even be able to afford some stands for spectators to sit in!

Suddenly, the referee blew her whistle. The game was about to start!

The two captains were shaking hands, whilst the referee placed a coin on top of her fist. But before she could flip the coin, an outraged shout stopped her.

'Stop! Stop right this instance!'

'Uh oh,' Mimi muttered, knocking her shoulder against Leah's. 'We've got company.'

Leah couldn't help the groan of dismay that slipped past her lips at the sight of Mr Smelting. He barged his way through the spectators, leaving a chorus of strangled protests in his wake, before coming to a halt in front of Edie.

'Ms Partridge, what on earth do you think you're doing?' he demanded, his nasal voice rising to an indignant, furious squeak. 'This . . . this farce is an outrage! It's preposterous! More than anything, it's illegal!'

'Actually, Mr Smelting,' Edie replied, her tone cool and her face expressionless. 'There's nothing illegal about it.'

Mr Smelting puffed himself up. If he'd been a bird, Leah imagined that all of his feathers would have been standing upright in some kind of boisterous territorial display. 'How dare you? The official documentation *clearly* states that female football matches are *banned*. I knew you were a troublemaker, Ms Partridge, but I wouldn't have taken you for a criminal, too!'

Edie tipped her head to the side, one eyebrow scathingly arched. 'You might deem football unsuitable for women, but that doesn't change the fact that we can, and we *will*, play the sport that we love.' Mr Smelting spluttered indignantly, but Edie held up her hand, cutting off his objections with an affronted gurgle. 'We aren't on an official ground and this is not an official fixture. Just a friendly competition between two *excellent* football teams. The fact that those teams are made up of women — well, that's irrelevant.' She shrugged.

'Irrelevant?' Mr Smelting looked like a kettle about to steam to the boil. 'Don't think I don't see what you're doing, using this *façade* to disguise the fact you're really playing the match that my organisation banned. By all rights, every single shilling you make today belongs to the government. To keep it for yourself would be thievery of the most repulsive kind!' He pointed one quivering, skeletal finger towards the ticketing table, his lips uncurling into a maliciously triumphant smile.

Leah watched Mr Smelting's contorted features with puzzled curiosity. His whole body seemed to vibrate with passion. It was clear that he believed every word he was saying. Sadly, the thought crossed her mind that, once upon a time, he must have had a dream too. Just like Dot did, and Anna, and George, and Mimi, and . . . probably every person around them on the field. The image of the red and white scarves he'd knitted for Mrs Miller flashed through her memory. They'd been created with such care. Leah couldn't imagine the gnarled fingers in front of her creating such soft and delicate things. She was certain that his dream had never been full of so much anger and sadness. What had gone wrong?

Mr Smelting sneered at the team, and his glacial eyes landed on each and every player. 'I'll stand for this no longer,' he hissed, turning to the crowd behind him. Near the front was a police officer, his peaked cap and navy uniform marking him out. Mr Smelting beckoned him over imperiously. 'Officer!'

Leah looked at George and Mimi in alarm as the policeman made his way politely through the crowd and across the pitch towards them. Leah gulped. If Mr Smelting managed to convince the officer that the football match was illegal, everything they'd done would be for nothing!

'What seems to be the problem, sir?' The officer said in a deep, authoritative voice. He rested his hands confidently on the shiny baton shoved through his belt.

Mr Smelting gestured at the team, loathing clear on his features. 'We require your services. An arrest – well, several arrests – need to be made. The integrity and respectability of this town is being gravely threatened.'

The policeman turned towards the team. Edie straightened her shoulders, standing tall and meeting his gaze in challenge.

Eventually the officer gave a reluctant nod and, with a sigh, unhooked a pair of silver handcuffs. 'You're right, sir,' he said. 'An offence has occurred.'

Leah's stomach sank. They'd worked so hard to pull off this match – they'd even caught a thief in the process! – and now it was all going to be ruined because of Mr Smelting. She felt her body tense as the policeman leaned forward and snapped the handcuffs closed.

On Mr Smelting's wrists.

'What is the meaning of this?' the tall official raged, tugging his hands uselessly against the metal restraints.

'Sir,' the police officer declared, 'the only one threatening the integrity of this town is you. I can't speak for everyone, but we're right proud of our ladies' team and they deserve the chance to play just as much as you and I. Now, if you'll

just come with me, we'll pop you somewhere you can't cause any more trouble.'

The team let out a great cheer as the officer marched a struggling Mr Smelting away. Even when they could no longer see him, they could still hear his shouted protests and weak threats.

'Will he go to jail?' George asked.

Edie shook her head. 'No, he hasn't really done anything wrong. Officer Stumpy will just make sure he doesn't come back onto the property and disrupt the match. Speaking of which . . .' She turned back to the referee, a glint shining in her eye, 'Let's get this game going!'

CHAPTER 29:
THE MATCH

After wishing the players good luck, the children hurried to the benches outside the changing rooms, brimming with trepidation. Mary was there too, but they scooted as far away from her as they could get, ignoring her sulky glares.

On the pitch, the referee finally flipped the coin. It soared high into the air, above their heads, before landing amongst the freshly cut grass. The three women peered over it, and then the referee pointed towards the Crickle End goal, where Sarah jumped about.

'Yes!' Mimi cheered. 'We've got the first kick!'

A short, sharp cry of the whistle sounded across the field, and then they were off! Edie passed the ball to Lizzie, and Leah watched in amazement as the team zoomed across the grass, the football little more than a blur as they weaved around defenders.

'This is going to be close,' Dot murmured as a Whitebridge player stole the ball from the Crickle End Champions, charging towards the goal at the other end of the pitch. 'The other team is really good!'

Leah had to agree. So far, it was impossible to tell which of the two teams was better, and as the game progressed it became clear how evenly matched they were. Within the first twenty minutes the Whitebridge Ladies managed two shots at the goal, but Sarah was too good for them. She caught each one almost effortlessly, much to the delight of the Crickle End supporters.

But it couldn't last forever. Leah gasped as a Whitebridge player dodged around a Crickle End defender. She swung her foot back, booting the ball powerfully towards the goal. Sarah jumped to catch it, but her arms weren't long enough. It hit the back of the net with an impressive swoosh. The Whitebridge supporters roared with elation, their players jumping up and down. Leah groaned, her hands on her head. On the pitch, the Crickle End players looked dejected, their shoulders slumped. It had been an amazing goal. Leah wasn't sure they could have done anything to stop it.

'Come on, Crickle End!' George suddenly roared from the bench next to her. He jumped to his feet, fists punching the air. Mimi leapt up to join him, her own bellows of encouragement echoing across the green. Soon, the crowd had taken up their cries too. Their chants of 'Crickle End! Crickle End!' were so loud they drowned out the celebrations of the opposing team.

On the pitch the players rallied, clapping each other on the back as the referee restarted play. With another burst from the whistle, they were off. Leah leaned forward on the bench, her heart hammering as the Crickle End Champions fought to gain an advantage.

But when the halftime whistle blew, the Whitebridge Ladies were still leading.

'Their defence is like iron!' Lizzie complained as they gathered around the benches for their team talk. Leah shuffled along the bench so she was closer to them and could better hear what they were saying.

Edie shook her head in disagreement. 'We're wearing them down, I can feel it. We just need to keep pushing.' She hit her fist into her palm. 'Don't let them get to you, team. We can win this!'

The players all gave determined nods before sprinting back onto the field.

When the second half started, the Crickle End Champions attacked with a renewed vigour. It seemed to take the Whitebridge Ladies by surprise and they flailed under the increased pressure. It was no shock to anyone when Edie won the ball and sent it flying into the bottom left corner, right through the goalkeeper's legs.

Leah sprang to her feet, screaming and waving her hands in the air. Mimi and George jumped along beside her, whilst Dot danced around in a jubilant circle. Next to them, Mary's scowl became even darker and she crossed her arms, hunching over moodily. The field was a riot of celebration.

Conceding a goal seemed to wake the Whitebridge Ladies from their halftime daze. They set their shoulders and their challenges became more aggressive as they fought to win the ball back. Leah gasped as Edie stumbled, Molly nipping in front of her to snatch the ball away. With only a handful of minutes until the end of the match, the opposing captain charged up the pitch towards the Crickle End goal. Sarah bounced around on the balls of her feet, ready to intercept Molly's strike. She darted forward, her hands outstretched in front of her. She was so fixated on the oncoming challenge that she didn't see Jo racing forward too. They collided with a crash, Molly tripping over their tangled limbs and sending the ball shooting off to the left. The referee blew hard on her whistle.

'Oh no!' Dot gasped, her hands over her mouth. Leah grimaced. Jo was rolling around, clutching her ankle, and it looked like Sarah was out cold.

'I can help!' Leah hadn't noticed Anna standing behind her, but now the older girl grabbed the medical bag from beneath the bench and sprinted across the field towards the players, her expression determined.

Leah watched as she crouched down beside them, her hands fluttering across the players' injuries. Edie loomed over her, features twisted in concern. Finally, Anna looked up at her, shaking her head.

'They're going to have to come off!' Mimi murmured. 'But who will Edie replace them with?' The girls eyed the bench. The only person sat on it beside them was a surly-looking Mary.

Anna helped a groggy Sarah off the pitch, whilst Edie came behind, supporting Jo, who was limping. Behind them, the two teams split off into separate huddles, taking the opportunity to grab a drink and discuss last-minute tactics.

Edie grimaced. 'We're a defender and a goalkeeper short. We can't continue with only nine players.'

'But you can't stop now!' Leah blurted.

Edie shot her a grim look. 'I don't know if I have much choice. There's no one . . . at least, no one I trust . . . ' Her eyes flicked to Mary but then she stopped abruptly, her eyes landing on Leah and Dot. 'Unless . . . what about you two? I know you're a bit young, but we're desperate. Do you think you could step in and help us out?'

'Me?' Leah squeaked.

'Absolutely!' Dot shouted, punching her fist in the air.

But Leah was shaking her head. 'No way. Sorry, Edie, but I can't.'

'What are you talking about, L?' Mimi cajoled. 'You're one of the best players on the team back home!'

'Yeah, but that's not like this. This is different.'

Edie's expression was beseeching. 'I know you're nervous, Leah, but we need you. If you don't agree to play for us, well, we'll need to forfeit the match!'

Leah didn't want that, but her stomach quivered at the thought of playing football in front of all these people. What if she wasn't good enough? What if she let the team down? Finally, she said, 'I'm not a defender like Jo.'

'That's okay!' Edie assured her. 'Lizzie can drop back into defence, and you can play up front with me.'

'Come on, Leah!' Dot urged, her face split by a wide grin. 'You can do this!' Could she? Looking around at her friends, Leah realised she was out of excuses. Besides, it *would* be really cool to play in a match like this one. She'd be like a real professional footballer. Swallowing her nerves and trying to be brave, she summoned a shaky smile. 'Okay,' she said. 'I'll do it.'

Edie beamed at her. 'I knew I could count on you, Leah!'

'Here,' said George, thrusting one wad of white fabric at her and another at Dot. 'These are for you.'

Leah shook out the bundle. It was a football

shirt. Written on the back in black marker pen was her name.

'There are some spare shorts and boots in the changing room too,' Edie told her, and she and Dot rushed inside to change.

When they emerged, they looked just like real members of the team.

'Wow,' Mimi gushed. 'You guys look great!'

'Are you ready to win this match?' Edie asked them. 'We've only got five minutes left, so we're going to have to make every second count!'

Leah and Dot jogged onto the pitch after her, leaving George and Mimi hooting on the sidelines. Leah followed Edie to the right while Dot sprinted towards the Crickle End goal. From where Leah was standing, Dot looked tiny in the middle of the goalposts, the space around her yawning. She felt a stab of anxiety. Could they really do this?

But there was no time for her to think about it any longer. The referee blew her whistle and the game started afresh. The ball weaved between the players, each side struggling to take control.

In the end, it was the Whitebridge Ladies who seized the first chance. One of their strikers intercepted a Crickle End pass, turning her body and angling it towards the goal. The muscles in Leah's shoulders tensed as the player kicked the ball. It arced towards the goal.

In the blink of an eye, Dot was there. She jumped so high she almost seemed to defy gravity, and then she rolled to the floor, the ball clasped safely between her gloved palms. Leah punched her fist into the air, roaring along with the crowd. Lizzie helped Dot to her feet, her expression jubilant as she thumped her on the back. Dot's smile transformed her face and her cheeks turned pink with pleasure.

When the referee blew her whistle, Dot booted the football into the air and Edie caught it on her chest. Bouncing it down to her feet, she ran towards the Whitebridge goal, her arms pumping as she charged down the side of the pitch, dodging every player that came her way. Leah watched her progress, silently urging her on.

Suddenly, Edie's head came up, her eyes searching. They landed on Leah. She called her name, pulling her foot back and passing the ball straight towards her.

Leah's heart thumped as she caught the ball with the side of her foot. A distant part of her mind registered that this was it, this could be a chance for her to win the game . . . But she didn't have time to focus on that; not with the burly defender that was coming straight towards her, her only aim to steal the ball and boot it away from the goal.

Leah came to life. Quicker than she thought possible, she spun around, taking the ball with her and dodging the defender's immense form. The crowd cheered as she charged towards the goal. Adrenaline rushed through her veins, exhilaration seemingly made her legs move faster. Her heart thumped with joy and suddenly everything felt right. This, she realised, was why Edie and the team had fought so hard to keep playing.

The goal loomed ahead of her. Before, Leah might have found the darting movements of the goalkeeper intimidating, but not any longer. She swung her foot back, her eyes trained on the back of the net, just like Edie had taught her, and kicked with all her might.

Excitement surged in Leah's stomach as the ball arced towards the top left corner . . . but then, out of nowhere, the defender Leah had dodged was there, deflecting the ball and sending the shot wide. The crowd groaned as Leah's stomach dropped. *She'd missed.* That had been their best chance and she'd wasted it. Dismay crashed through her.

A piercing whistle sounded, jerking Leah from her disappointment. The ref, whistle perched between her lips, was pointing at the penalty spot!

'What's going on?' Leah asked, as Edie jogged towards her with the ball in her hands, grinning wildly.

'It was a handball! The ref is giving us a penalty!'

Leah gave a *whoop*, echoing the excitement of the crowd around her. So it wasn't over yet! They still had one last chance.

She watched as Edie placed the ball on the penalty spot. For a split second, Leah wished she was the one preparing to take the shot that could win or lose them the game. She thought back to the penalty shoot-out in Miss Kaur's training session. Leah had changed so much since then, and she'd learned more about herself and what she was capable of. Wasn't this the perfect chance to prove that?

Before she could stop herself, Leah jogged towards Edie. 'I know there's a lot riding on this but . . . can I take the penalty?'

The captain looked down at her, one eyebrow arched. 'This is our only chance to win, Leah. It's a big responsibility. Are you sure you're ready?'

Was she? Brushing the doubts away, Leah nodded. 'I can do this, Edie.'

Edie stared at her for a moment longer and then she smiled. With a flourish, she gestured towards the penalty spot. 'It's all yours.'

There was a shocked murmur from the crowd as Leah stepped up, but she didn't listen. Instead, she focused on keeping her breathing calm as she got into position. In the goal, the Whitebridge keeper jumped left and right, but Leah ignored her. Her focus was entirely on the ball at her feet. *She could do this.*

With a sharp inhale, Leah ran towards the ball. The crowd seemed to lean forward in anticipation as her foot connected with it, and then it was flying through the air, between the hands of the goalkeeper and into the back of the net with a triumphant *swoosh!*

The crowd went wild. The Crickle End Champions charged towards her. Over the din, the referee blew the whistle, signalling the end of the game. They'd done it! They'd won! Leah suddenly felt herself being lifted and a small hand gripped hers as Dot, too, was hoisted onto the players' shoulders. The air rang with the sound of their names being chanted. 'Leah! Leah! Dot! Dot!'

Leah smiled so hard that her cheeks started to ache.

CHAPTER 30:
A WAY HOME

When Edie lifted the Championship Cup high above her head, the crowd bellowed its delight, thousands of feet stamping the ground in unison. She passed it to Leah, its bulbous body gleaming gold in the morning light. Gripping one handle, Leah offered the other to Dot and they lifted the trophy together, the buoyant celebrations of their friends echoing in their ears. The team gathered around them, each one with identical smiles stretching right across their cheeks.

'Leah! Look over here!' George's voice cut through the noise, and Leah turned to see her friend pushing his way to the front of the crowd. He had his camera held up against his eye and he pressed the shutter, capturing her and

Dot holding the trophy high.

It took a long time for the field to empty and even longer for the team to make their way back across the pitch towards the changing room.

'Phew!' Dot said, putting the trophy down on the bench. She flexed her wrist. 'That thing is heavier than it looks.'

'You guys were amazing!' Jo bubbled from where she was sitting, her ankle elevated, with an ice pack resting on top of it.

'It was a team effort really,' Leah said, her cheeks flushing.

'No, Jo's right,' Edie chimed in, placing a hand on both Leah and Dot's shoulders. 'You saved us in our hour of need *and* you won the Championship for us. We couldn't have done it without you.'

'Hey!' George shouted suddenly. 'Maybe this means...' his voice trailed off as he looked furtively at Edie and Lizzie, who were now engaged in an intense conversation about different strategies they could try for next season.

'Means what?' Mimi prompted.

'Come here,' George beckoned them away from the adults. Once they were no longer in earshot, he leaned towards them. 'Maybe helping the team win was what the watch wanted us to do. Maybe now we can go home?'

'The watch!' Leah exclaimed. She spun around, her eyes landing on Mary. With the excitement of the match, she hadn't had a chance to ask the older woman to give it back.

Mimi and George followed Leah as she marched over to the bench, Dot coming more slowly behind them. Mary scowled at them as they approached.

'Mary,' George said before Leah could open her mouth. 'We know you stole our watch, and we want it back, right now.' Mimi and Leah exchanged a look of surprise. They'd never heard George sound so bold before.

'I don't know what you're talking about, you little brat,' Mary spat. She sniffed and turned her face away from them, her arms folded firmly across her chest.

'Isn't it a bit late to play innocent?' Mimi asked

primly, one eyebrow arched. 'Everyone already knows you're a thief.'

Mary's head whipped round and she opened her mouth to reply, but before she could, Anna's voice interrupted. 'Mary's telling the truth.' She stepped up behind her sister, who refused to look in her direction. 'We don't know anything about a watch.'

'But . . . but if you didn't take it, who did?' Leah's voice was full of dismay.

'Um . . .' Dot's voice was quiet. She stepped forward, her hand outstretched. In her palm was the pocket watch. 'It was me.'

'Dot!' Leah exclaimed, taking the watch. 'Why would you do something like that? You know how important that watch is to us!'

'I'm sorry!' Dot cried, her face crumpling. 'I know I shouldn't have taken it, but I was so scared it would send you all back home before we'd had a chance to work out who was trying to sabotage the team. I wouldn't have been able to solve it on my own. I needed you! When I saw it lying on top of George's coat the other day in training . . . I couldn't stop myself.'

'So you stole from us and kept us here even when we were desperate to get home,' Mimi accused, her voice hard.

'You didn't even believe us when we told you about the watch's magic,' George whispered, leaning forward. He shot a furtive look at Mary and Anna, but they weren't listening. Anna was trying to talk to her sister, but Mary was stubbornly quiet, her eyes staring straight ahead.

'If you'd just asked us, we would have stayed,' Mimi huffed angrily.

Dot bowed her head, hugging her arms across her chest. 'I know,' she said, her voice small. 'I shouldn't have done it.' Her bottom lip trembled.

Leah stepped forward, her hand landing on

Dot's shoulder. She frowned. 'She clearly realises it was a mistake.'

Dot looked up, her eyes wide. 'You're not angry at me?'

Leah shrugged. 'I'm not pleased, but I understand why you did it. Besides, it's not like you kept it. Holding a grudge never helps anyone. At least, that's what my mum always says.' She shrugged and gave Dot a small smile. 'I forgive you. We all do, don't we, guys?' She looked meaningfully at the others.

George nodded, but Mimi's frown deepened. After a second, though, she rolled her eyes and gave a reluctant smile. 'Fine!' she relented. 'We forgive you.'

Dot smiled broadly, her eyes shining. 'You guys are the best friends I've ever had,' she said.

'Oh, stop it,' Mimi laughed. She rushed forward, drawing her into a massive hug. After a second, George piled in too, and Leah wrapped her arms around them all, laughing. She felt like her heart was full enough to burst.

CHAPTER 31: TIME TO SAY GOODBYE

'What do we do now?' Mimi finally said, pulling back and brushing her braids away from her face.

'Well, now that the match has been such a success, and we have the watch back, I guess we should try to see if we can get home.'

'Oh,' Dot said, in a melancholy voice. 'Do you have to?'

'We'd love to stay, but . . .'

'You want to go home, I know,' Dot sighed, resigned. She gestured towards the players who were still congregating around the changing room. 'We should probably go somewhere a bit quieter before we test it out. What about the churchyard? No one will see us there.'

Leah nodded in agreement. 'Although, maybe

we could get changed first?' She plucked at her white football shirt, which was now covered in faint grass stains. The shorts weren't much cleaner.

Leaving George, Mimi and Rolo outside, Leah and Dot flew into the changing room. It didn't take long for them to shimmy out of their kits, throwing their dresses and tights on as fast as they could. Leah folded up the shorts neatly, placing them on the bench with the boots next to them. She lingered over the shirt, though, her fingers rubbing the fabric thoughtfully.

'You should keep that,' Dot said as she laced up her boots.

'Do you think so?'

Dot nodded firmly. 'Absolutely. It'll remind you that, no matter what, your dreams are always within reach if you just stretch out your hand. Besides, you earned it.'

Leah grinned and slid the shirt into her backpack.

Outside, George was busy clicking photos of Mimi and Rolo as they capered around on the grass. When Leah and Dot appeared he straightened up, tucking the photos away into his pocket.

'Ready?' he said.

'You're not leaving so soon, are you?'

Leah whirled as Edie came to a stop beside her. The captain's cheeks were a merry red and the exhilaration of their win sparkled in her dark eyes.

'It's time for us to go home,' Leah said.

'Well, before you leave, I just want to say again how grateful we are. If it wasn't for you, we never would have caught Mary and we definitely wouldn't have won that match.' Edie extended her hand to Leah. 'You kids did us a real favour both times. You're like some kind of wonder team.'

'Hey!' Mimi piped up. 'The Wonder Team! I like that!'

Leah laughed and pressed her palm against Edie's, shaking her hand with a grin. 'You would have figured it all out eventually. We just helped you along.'

'You should come and play for us again, Leah. We could use someone with your skill. Plus, we're going to need another striker for our new goalkeeper to practise against.' Edie winked at Dot.

Dot's eyes widened and she clapped her hands together. 'Me? Do you mean it, Edie?'

Edie shrugged. 'You'll still need to wait until you're a bit older to be a permanent starter, but after a performance like today, I'd be an idiot not to at least have you on the bench.'

Letting out an excited squeal, Dot rushed at the captain, flinging her arms around her waist with such force that Edie nearly fell backwards. 'Oh, thank you, thank you, thank you! I won't let you down!'

Edie laughed, patting Dot's head affectionately. She glanced at Leah. 'So, what do you say? Can we count on you for the next game?'

Leah's smile faded as she glanced at George and Mimi. Sadly, she shook her head. 'I'd love that, but we won't be sticking around for much longer. We've got to get . . . back to the circus.

They'll be leaving soon.' At the last minute, she remembered the white lie they'd told the team about where they'd come from.

Edie shrugged regretfully. 'That's a shame. If you ever do pass through Crickle End again, though, make sure you come and find us! You'll always have a home here.' She paused, her eyes darting over to a rigid figure on the bench. 'Now, if you'll excuse me, I've got some team business to deal with before any of us can go home.' She marched over to where Mary was sitting, her hands set firmly on her hips.

'What will happen to Mary?' Leah asked as the four of them set off across the field after waving goodbye to the still-celebrating football team. Rolo loped along at Mimi's side and she ruffled his ears affectionately.

'Will they report her to the police?' George chipped in.

Dot shook her head. 'I know Mary's a thief, but Edie won't get the authorities involved. Like I said this morning, the team are like a family. The players are angry, but they won't cast her out. Anyway, there are better ways for Mary to make up for what she's done.' Dot gave a sly smile. 'Like washing boots and picking up clean kits. She thinks she's so much better than the rest of us, so she'll hate that.'

They crossed the road, and Dot led them towards a gate that opened into the small churchyard. The spire of the church soared above them, its pointed tip reaching towards the clouds. The shadows of the graves below had almost disappeared as the sun edged towards its midpoint in the sky.

As they traversed the narrow path, George asked, 'What about Anna? Do you think she'll get to live her dream and become a doctor?'

Dot shrugged. 'Who knows? Edie will do everything she can to help her.' Her face brightened. 'The team could always use a regular medic to help out at our matches.'

Suddenly, a loud, melodic *bong* rolled across the churchyard as the bells in the tower began to ring. It was so loud, Leah could feel the vibrations through her plimsolls.

Mimi stopped abruptly, lifting her face up to the tower. 'Those bells . . . does that mean it's almost midday?'

Shading her eyes as she stared up at the church, Dot nodded. 'I think so,' she said, her voice reluctant.

Leah fished out the watch from where she'd stashed it in her pocket. The two black hands were standing to attention, pointing at the Roman numeral for twelve. As she stared, it looked like they quivered with impatience, the metal casing warming alarmingly in her palm.

'Guys,' Leah said, showing them the watch face. 'I think the watch is trying to tell us that it's time to go home.'

'This is really it, then,' Mimi said mournfully, rubbing her hands over Rolo's head. He butted up against her, his tail wagging.

A heavy silence fell between them, the bells tolling urgently in the background.

'Will I ever see you again?' Dot suddenly blurted.

Leah, Mimi and George exchanged uneasy

glances. If the watch did work, it would catapult them back to the future. There was no knowing whether it would ever bring them back.

Finally, Leah forced a smile. 'Who knows where the watch will take us? We could be back before you know it.'

'Oh!' George cried. He reached into his pocket, pulling out his stack of photos. Quickly, he flipped through them until he found the one he was after and, smiling broadly, he turned it towards the others.

The picture showed the four of them at the circus, beaming up at the camera where George had angled it above them. In the bottom-left corner, Rolo's wet nose and gleaming black eyes were just visible.

'You can keep that to remember us by,' George said, handing the photo to Dot and rubbing one hand through his messy curls.

Dot blinked rapidly, her eyes bright. She hugged the photograph against her chest. 'Thank you, George.' Her voice sounded thick, as though she were trying not to cry. 'I'll treasure it forever.'

Rolo gave a *woof* of agreement, excitably turning in a circle at Mimi's feet. She dropped to her knees, wrapping her arms around his neck.

'Will you look after Rolo, too, Dot? I don't want him going back on the streets after we're gone.' She buried her head in his curly ears.

'I promise,' Dot replied. She hooked her fingers into Rolo's red collar and pulled him to sit at her feet. Rolo went reluctantly, giving a little whine as Mimi stood up and stepped away.

'We'd better hurry,' Leah said, glancing up at the tower. 'The bells won't last forever. We've only got a few more before they stop. Quick, grab hold.' She thrust the watch forward and Mimi and George leaned in, placing their fingers against the shining metal.

'We'll never forget you, Dot,' Leah called, and then, before she could change her mind, she clicked the crown twice.

Just as she did, Rolo suddenly gave an enthusiastic bark, breaking free from Dot's grip. As time slowed, and the world began to dance and whirl, the small spaniel leapt towards them, straight for Mimi's outstretched arm.

Everything melted into a dizzying blend of purple and blue as the children plunged forward into a spinning silver void.

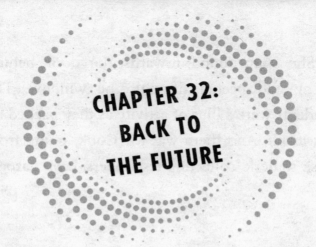

CHAPTER 32: BACK TO THE FUTURE

When they landed this time, Leah didn't stumble. She braced herself and planted her legs as her feet hit the floor. Next to her, George wasn't so lucky. He tipped backwards, landing onto his bottom with an *oomph*.

As Mimi helped him to his feet, Leah blinked, looking around her. They were back in the school corridor, the door to the history classroom right behind them. There was a shrill ringing in the air, and Leah realised they'd returned just as the school bell had gone.

That was odd, when they'd been whisked away the first time, the bell had also been ringing. Leah frowned, looking down at the watch clutched in her fist. Unless . . .

She spun round towards the door behind them, and peered through the window. The students were a blur of activity as they packed up for lunch. And there was Mr Cook, going from desk to desk, collecting test papers. Leah gasped.

'We're back right where we started!' she exclaimed.

'What?' said George, dusting off his trousers.

'We were in the past for three days, but no time has gone by at all here!' Leah replied, pointing through the classroom window. 'Look, that's the history test we sat on Tuesday. Or is it today? This is confusing.' Leah shook her head and giggled.

'You're right!' Mimi exclaimed. 'Mr Cook is wearing the exact same tie and jacket.'

'That means we haven't missed the match against Westfield High,' Leah said gleefully.

'Time travel is so weird,' George sighed, rubbing his forehead.

A bark rang out, as if in agreement. Rolo! He was prancing around their feet, his curly, toffee-coloured ears bouncing around his muzzle. Mimi cried out and dropped to her knees, hugging the little spaniel close.

'Rolo! What are you doing here?'

'He jumped at you,' Leah said, her mind dancing back to the split second after she pressed the crown when the little dog had broken out of Dot's grasp. 'The watch must have brought him back through with us.'

'Oh dear,' Mimi laughed. 'Mum and Dad are going to go crazy when I bring you home.' Rolo licked her face, his pink tongue swiping up and across her nose. Mimi giggled.

'I'm not sure it's your mum and dad you've got to worry about, Mimi,' George said, a note of warning in his voice. 'We've got bigger problems.' He pointed through the classroom door. Their classmates were heading their way and so was Mr Cook.

'Quick, hide him behind our legs!' Leah ushered the others into a semi-circle against the wall, with Rolo ensconced in the middle. Leah shoved the watch into her dress pocket.

Luckily, doors began to fly open up and down the corridor as students left their lessons, heading towards the cafeteria. The burble of their conversation covered most of Rolo's excitable yaps. When Mr Cook marched into the corridor, looming over them, he didn't so much as glance at Rolo's hiding place.

An almighty scowl creased the history teacher's forehead as he stared down at them all. His top lip curled in disapproval. Leah suddenly realised that, even though they looked nothing alike, he reminded her of Mr Smelting.

'Well, what have you three got to say for yourselves?' He held up an impatient hand, stopping their answers. 'No, don't speak. You might not think the history of our world has any bearing on your life, but I can tell you with absolute certainty that it's one of the most important subjects you'll ever take,' Mr Cook droned. His voice had an air of lecturing about it, and Leah fought down a sigh. At least when they'd been living in the past, they hadn't had to put up with this.

Mr Cook was still going. 'We can learn valuable lessons from the past, lessons that will inform the decisions we have yet to make. One small act can change everything. Don't you realise—' he suddenly broke off, his eyes narrowing as he looked between them. 'What on earth are you wearing?'

The three of them stared down at their clothes. They were still wearing everything that Dot had let them borrow!

'Uh . . .'

'It's for drama class!' Mimi blurted. 'We have a rehearsal during lunch and we thought changing now would save time.'

Leah internally breathed a sigh of relief. Thank goodness for Mimi and her quick thinking.

At that moment, Rolo decided he'd had enough of being hidden away. With a joyful bark, he slipped through Mimi's legs, his tail wagging energetically as he bounded around their feet. With a playful growl, the small spaniel leapt up at Mr Cook, tongue ready to deliver a soggy kiss. Mr Cook gave a cry of alarm, raising his hands, but that only made it easier for Rolo to plant his paws on his knees and push. The two of them landed in a heap on the corridor floor, Mr Cook's arms and legs flailing as he pushed against Rolo's wet nose.

'Rolo!' Mimi shouted, jumping forward to pull him away.

'Uh oh,' Leah muttered to George as Mimi dragged Rolo back, their history teacher heaving himself to his feet. His face was puce with anger. 'Maybe we should have stayed in 1921 after all!'

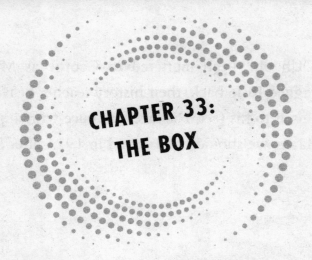

CHAPTER 33:
THE BOX

Leah, Mimi and George left Rolo in the school office, sitting politely at the foot of the receptionist's desk. They waved goodbye and he wagged his tail happily. Behind him, Mr Cook's complexion was becoming alarmingly scarlet as he gripped the phone to his ear, arguing with Mimi's mum, who was adamant that she didn't need to come to the school to pick up her dog because she didn't *have* one.

As the three of them wandered towards the cafeteria, Mimi chewed on her thumbnail. 'I hope Mum does come and get Rolo,' she said. 'What if she says I can't keep him?'

George patted her shoulder. 'I'm sure she will. She might put up a bit of a fight, but we all know you and your mum are pretty much the same when it comes to dogs. Complete suckers.'

They laughed as they weaved their way through the crowd of students, collected their lunch from the hot counter and settled themselves at a free table by the window. For a moment, there was silence as they all picked at their food.

'No one would ever believe us if we told them about the last couple of days,' George suddenly said.

'Which is why we'll have to keep it a complete secret,' Leah announced. She drew the watch from her pocket, placing it in the middle of the table. They all leaned forward to stare at it. Experimentally, Leah reached out her hand and pressed the crown twice. Nothing happened, but then, Leah hadn't really expected anything to.

'I wonder what happened to them all,' Mimi mused. 'Dot and Anna and Edie. Even Mary. Do you think their dreams came true?'

Leah hoped so. 'Maybe we can find out,' she suggested. 'My dad's always going on about how good the library is. He told me they've got loads of old newspapers. We could search for clues in there?'

Mimi beamed. 'Good idea, L!'

The mention of Mary made Leah's mind drift to the disastrous training session they'd had before the watch had transported them to the past. Just like the star striker, William had done his best to sabotage her chance to show what she was made of. Well, she decided, curling her hands into determined fists, next time, he wouldn't succeed.

'What are we going to do with the watch, now?' Mimi tapped the clock's glass face. 'Should we bury it under the tree again?'

Leah shook her head. 'I don't think so. I feel like the watch wanted us to find it. The note said it all. It's for those that need it most. The watch chose us. We're its keepers now.'

George nodded. 'Maybe we can take turns looking after it.'

'Good idea, George. I'll put it back in the box, though, just to keep it safe.' Leah pulled her backpack up to the bench, rooting around until she found the metal case jammed right at the bottom.

As she lifted it out of the bag, she noticed it felt heavier than it had, and when she placed it on the table, something rattled around inside.

'What's that?' Mimi asked. 'Did you put something else in there?'

'Nothing,' Leah replied, shaking her head in confusion. 'I haven't opened it since we found it at the tree.' Her fingers fumbled over the open padlock and she slid it through the catch, flipping the lid open. The three of them leaned forward, peering into the black opening of the box.

Leah tilted her head. 'Is that . . .?'

'It's a compass!' Mimi cried, reaching in and pulling out the circular disc and displaying it on her palm. 'My dad has one just like it that he uses when he goes hiking! Although, this one is much prettier.'

At first glance it looked like a metal clam, a silver hinged lid standing at a right angle to the main body of the compass. Leah thought it seemed very similar to the watch. It, too, had a glass surface, surrounded by filigree etchings, with a cream face beneath, but instead of numbers around the outside there were letters, one for each cardinal point. A single red needle quivered, spinning from side to side as Mimi moved her hand.

'Where did it come from?' George asked, staring into the box as if it would reveal the answer to his question.

Leah looked too. The compass definitely hadn't been there when they'd opened the box before, but somehow, between then and now, it had appeared.

'The box must be magic too,' she announced finally, shutting the lid and holding it up to the light. She examined it from every angle, but no matter how she looked at it, it was still just a battered, metal box.

'Why's it appeared now?' Mimi said. 'Do you think the box has sent it to us for a reason? Like it sent us the watch?'

Leah shrugged. She took the compass from Mimi's hand and placed it on the table next to the watch. 'I'm not sure,' she said. She shot them an excited smile. 'But I have a feeling it means our adventures aren't over just yet.'

CHAPTER 34: TEAM WONDER

The team clustered around the bench in silence, the air tense. Nervously, the players watched the spectators file into the stands. This was it, the big match against their rivals, Westfield High. In less than five minutes they'd be marching onto the pitch to take their positions.

Leah scanned the azure sky, trying to quell the butterflies fluttering agitatedly in her stomach. She was relieved to see that there wasn't a storm cloud in sight. It was the perfect kind of weather to accompany a spectacular win.

'Blimey,' Miss Kaur said, emerging from the changing room and dropping her sports bag onto one of the benches. She rubbed her hands together as she took in the drooped shoulders and uneasy expressions of her team. 'You lot look like you'd rather be anywhere else. What's wrong?'

The team shuffled uncomfortably, waiting for someone to say it. It was William Riley who finally plucked up the courage, his plump cheeks red and angry as he said, 'We don't stand a chance of winning this, Miss. We're rubbish!'

Miss Kaur put her hands on her hips, frowning. 'Rubbish? What makes you say that? You're an excellent team!'

'Our last match was a shambles!' William exclaimed. 'Our defence was a joke, and *someone* missed our winning goal.' He glared at Leah, but instead of looking away, she glared right back.

'You can't be perfect all the time,' Miss Kaur argued. 'This is a new game, a fresh slate, and you've been practising so hard. This is your chance to go out there and make right everything that went wrong last time. I've got faith that–' she broke off suddenly, her face twisting with annoyance as she looked over the team's shoulder. Someone was calling her name. Leah turned to look too. It was Mr Cook. He was holding a clipboard and seemed to be arguing with the referee about the position of the goalposts.

Miss Kaur sighed. 'Right in the middle of my pep talk, too,' she muttered, rubbing a hand across her forehead. She looked at the players. 'I'll be back in one moment,' she promised, before dashing forward to intercept a very angry Mr Cook, who was now waving his arms – and the clipboard – above his head dramatically.

Leah looked at her teammates. It was like all of the positivity had been sucked out of them. That was no good; they hadn't even started the game yet. How were they supposed to win when they believed it was impossible?

Before she had time to really think about what she was doing, Leah stepped forward.

William groaned and rolled his eyes. 'Great,' he muttered, then said sarcastically, 'are you going to give us your best tips on how to lose a game in style?'

'Shut up, William!' Mimi seethed.

'It's okay, Mimi,' Leah said. She thought of Edie and the way she'd been so calm when she spoke to the Crickle End Champions. The memory of the cool and collected captain soothed her nerves, and she found herself standing up straighter. She could do this. She levelled her gaze at William, willing her confidence to shine through. He suddenly went quiet, his expression unsure. He swallowed noisily and took a step back.

Leah looked directly at her teammates with an encouraging smile. 'This might seem like the worst thing to say before the biggest and most

important match we've ever played, but football *isn't* the most important thing in the world.' A few players raised their eyebrows, exchanging doubtful glances. Leah ignored them and forced herself to press on. 'Or, at least, that's what people will try to tell you. They'll say that it's just a game, but for us, it's more than that. All of us love playing football. We wouldn't do it if we didn't. It's what we're passionate about and, really, we're lucky that we're allowed to play whenever we want to. There are so many forgotten footballers of the past that didn't get the recognition they deserved. But things are different now.'

They were all staring at her, listening intently. Even William was leaning forward slightly, his mouth ajar. Feeling her confidence grow even more, Leah gestured at the pitch behind them. 'I could stand here and lecture you about all the drills and practice that we've done as a team to help us reach this point, but I don't need to. I know that each and every one of you is good enough to go out there and win this game. We just need to stick together. We're a team, and we should support each other, off the pitch and on it. We might go out there today and lose. That would suck, but it would be okay because we'd have done it together as a team. I don't believe that's going to happen, though,' she paused, then grinned wide. 'When you love football as much as we do, there's no way we can be beaten!' She threw her hands in the air as the team cheered and shouted around her, stomping their feet on the grass.

Leah gave a firm nod, and then, grinning in anticipation, she led her team out onto the pitch.

The End.

THE DICK, KERR LADIES

Although the Crickle End Champions weren't a real football team, they were inspired by an incredible group of people who helped women's football become popular before it was banned in 1921: the *Dick, Kerr Ladies F.C.* Here are some brilliant facts about that wonderful team:

⚽ *Dick, Kerr Ladies F.C.* was formed at the Dick, Kerr & Co munitions factory in Preston, England during the First World War in 1917. After beating a group of men during a lunchtime football match, the women decided to form a team and named themselves after the factory.

⚽ Their kit was a black and white striped shirt, like Newcastle United, with blue shorts. The players also wore hats to keep their hair out of the way.

⚽ On Christmas Day, 1917, *Dick, Kerr Ladies F.C.* played a charity match to help fundraise for

The Dick, Kerr Ladies F.C.

wounded soldiers. They raised £600, which is the same as £50,000 in today's money!

⚽ Three years later, on Boxing Day 1920, almost 70,000 people travelled to Liverpool, to Goodison Park Stadium (now home to Everton FC) to watch *Dick, Kerr Ladies F.C.* play – and many fans were turned away as the ground was too full! This was to be the largest crowd for a women's football game for nearly 100 years and they won 4-0! Some people believe that the popularity of this match contributed to the FA's decision to ban women's football in 1921.

⚽ Lily Parr was one of their most famous players. She joined the team in 1920 when she was just 15 years old, and her kick was so strong that she once broke a man's arm when taking a penalty against him! She scored nearly 1000 goals before she stopped playing in 1951.

⚽ Even though women's football was banned from playing on official FA pitches in 1921, *Dick, Kerr Ladies F.C.* continued to play until 1965. They played 833 matches at home and internationally, only losing 28. The team celebrated their 100th anniversary in 2017 and were awarded a Special Recognition Award from the FA.

⚽ The ban on women's football was finally lifted 50 years later, in 1971.

ABOUT THE AUTHORS

Leah Williamson plays as a defender for Arsenal and the Lionesses, England Women's Football team. In the summer of 2022 Leah captained the Lionesses to victory in the UEFA Women's Euro 2022.

As the first captain in the men's or women's senior teams to lead England to a European victory, Leah is uniquely positioned to motivate and inspire younger generations, and her first book, *You Have the Power*, is an empowering guide for children.

Jordan Glover grew up with her nose perpetually lodged in a book. As an adult, living in Cambridgeshire with her husband, son, cat, and dog, not much has changed. When not searching for magic and adventure between the pages of her current read, you can find her scribbling away or studying for her masters in Creative Writing with the Open University. *The Wonder Team and the Forgotten Footballers* is her debut novel.

ABOUT THE ILLUSTRATOR

Robin Boyden is a freelance illustrator based in Herefordshire in the West of England. In 2007 he graduated from University College Falmouth with a First Class Honours Degree and soon after completed a Masters in Art and Design.

Robin works in the picture book and middle grade fiction market and has previously worked as an editorial illustrator. He has twice been selected for the AOI Images annual and has worked for numerous clients in the publishing and editorial sectors worldwide.

ACKNOWLEDGEMENTS

From Leah

To have been able to do this alongside my cousin, Jordan, has been a blessing. Thank you, Jordan, for bringing this story to life in a way I could never have dreamed of.

Thank you also to Tongue Tied and Macmillan for allowing us to try and inspire the next generation through a little bit of history.

Our family. From the minute the idea was spoken about at Tiffany Beach Club, your support and excitement have made this journey so fun and full of love!

Finally, thank you to the women that came before me, the pioneers of the women's game. I stand on your shoulders and I will continue to shine a light on your place in history.

From Jordan

This book wouldn't be here today without the hard work of so many people, least of all my cousin, Leah. Who knew this was where we'd end up when we were playing *Blind Date* in the back bedroom at Grandma's house? Thank you so much for going on this adventure with me and putting up with my relentless Whatsapp questions. We did it!

To everyone at Macmillan and Tongue Tied, thank you for your constant support and encouragement. Doing something like this can be scary but you made it easy for both of us. Your expertise has crafted this book into what it is and has given us the chance to show children everywhere that they can reach for their dreams no matter what.

My Take Twos. You've been a pillar of strength since I started this project. I'm so fortunate to have found such a talented group of writers who constantly challenge me to think in new ways and inspire me with their ideas and dreams.

Family has always been so important to both of us, and we're incredibly lucky to be surrounded by so much love and belief. You've made us into who we are today and you'll continue shaping us far into the future. We love you all.

And finally, to my husband, Rob, who has had to shoulder so much of the parenting burden whilst I've squirrelled myself away with my laptop. You never gave up on what you thought I could do, even when I doubted myself. In the words of Omi, I think that I found myself a cheerleader. You're always right there when I need you. Thank you.